HEROINES
OF ALL AGES

CO-EDITED BY
HAMILTON WRIGHT MABIE
AND KATE STEPHENS
DECORATED BY
BLANCHE OSTERTAG

ACKNOWLEDGMENTS

The editors and publishers wish to acknowledge the courtesy of authors and publishers named below, for the use of certain material in this volume: To Mrs. Elizabeth E. Seelye for material adapted for Pocahontas, from her volume entitled "Pocahontas" (copyrighted, 1879, by Dodd, Mead & Company); to Messrs. Harper and Brothers and to the Estate of Mr. John S.C. Abbott for material adapted for Madame Roland; to Messrs. Dodd, Mead & Company for material adapted for Alcestis, Antigone and Iphigenia; to Messrs. E.P. Dutton & Company for material adapted for Lady Jane Grey; to the Macmillan Company for certain material in Paula; to Messrs. Hutchinson & Company, London, for material adapted for Sister Dora.

INTRODUCTION

The Book of Heroes should never be separated from the Book of Heroines; they are the two parts of that story of courage, service and achievement which is the most interesting and inspiring chapter in the history of human kind in this wonderful world of ours. Whenever and wherever there has appeared a hero, a heroine has almost always worked with or for him; for heroic and noble deeds are rarely done without some kind of coöperation. Now and then, it is true, single acts of daring stand out alone; but, as a rule, the hero gains his end because other men or women stand beside him in times of great peril. William the Silent could not have made his heroic defence of the Low Countries against the armies of Spain if men of heroic temper and women of indomitable courage had not been about him in those terrible years; Washington could not have converted a body of farmers into an organized and disciplined army if he had not been aided by the skill of drill masters like Steuben; nor could Lieutenant Peary make brilliant dashes for the North Pole if other men did not join him in his perilous expeditions. The hero is generally a leader of heroes, as a great general is a leader of soldiers who carry out his plans in hourly jeopardy of limb and life.

It is a mistake to think of heroes as rare and exceptional men; the world is full of those who take their lives in their hands every day and think nothing about it; or, if they think of it at all, think of it, as Mr. Kipling would say, as part of the day's work. It is almost impossible to open a daily newspaper without coming upon some story of daring by some obscure man or woman. The record of a fire department is usually a continuous register of the brave deeds done by those who receive very small pay for a very dangerous service to their fellows. It is not necessary to go back to the days of chivalry or to open the histories of great wars to find a hero; he lives in every street, works in every profession and never thinks that he is doing anything unusual or impressive. There are many stories of heroic deeds and men, but these are as nothing compared with the unwritten stories of brave and chivalrous people whose lives are full of courage, self-denial and sacrifice, but of whom no public reports are ever made.

It has taken three centuries to explore and settle this country, and there are still parts of it in which those who live face the perils and hardships of pioneers. Ever since the war of the Revolution the skirmish line of civilisation has moved steadily forward from the Atlantic to the Pacific; and every man who has carried a rifle or an axe, who has defended his home against Indians or cut down trees, made a clearing, built a rude house and turned the prairie or the land taken from the forest into a farm, has had something of the hero in him. He has often been selfish, harsh and unjust; but he has been daring, full of endurance and with a capacity for heroic work; But he has never been alone; we see him always as he faces his foes or bears the strain of his work: we often forget that there was as much courage in the log house as on the firing line at the edge of the forest, and that the work indoors was harder in many ways than the work out of doors and far less varied and inspiriting. If we could get at the facts we should find that there have been more heroines than heroes in the long warfare of the race against foes within and without, and that the courage of women has had far less to stimulate it in dramatic or picturesque conditions or crises. It is much easier to make a perilous charge in full daylight, with flying banners and the music of bugles ringing across the field, than to hold a lonely post, in solitude at midnight, against a stealthy and unseen enemy.

Boys do not need to be taught to admire the bold rush on the enemies' position, the brilliant and audacious passage through the narrow channel under the guns of masked batteries, the lonely march into Central Africa, the dash to the North Pole; they do need to be taught the heroism of those who give the hero his sword and then go home to wait for his return; who leave the stockade unarmed and, under a fire of poisoned arrows, run to the springs for water for a thirsting garrison; who quietly stay at their posts and as quietly die without the inspiration of dramatic achievement or of the heart-felt applause of spectators; who bear heavy burdens without a chance to drop or change them; who are heroically patient under blighting disappointments and are loyal to those who are disloyal to them; who bear terrible wrongs in silence, and conceal the cowardice of those they love and cover their retreat with a smiling courage which is the very soul of the pathos of unavailing heroism and undeserved failure.

From the days of Esther, Judith and Antigone to those of Florence Nightingale, women have shown every kind of courage that men have shown, faced every kind of peril that men have braved, divided with men the dangers and hardships of heroism but have never had an equal share of recognition and applause. So far as they are concerned this lack of equal public reward has been of small consequence; the best of them have not only not cared for it, but have shunned it. It is well to remember that the noblest heroes have never sought applause; and that popularity is much more dangerous to heroes than the foes they faced or the savage conditions they mastered in the splendid hour of daring achievement. Many heroes have been betrayed by popularity into vanity and folly and have lost at home the glory they won abroad. Heroic women have not cared for public recognition and do not need it; but it is of immense importance to society that the ideals of heroism should be high and true, and that the soldier and the explorer should not be placed above those whose achievements have been less dramatic, but of a finer quality. The women who have shown heroic courage, heroic patience, heroic purity and heroic devotion outrank the men whose deeds have had their inspiration in physical bravery, who have led splendid charges in full view of the world, who have achieved miracles of material construction in canal or railroad, or the reclaiming of barbarous lands to the uses of civilization. In a true scale of heroic living and doing women must be counted more heroic than men.

A writer of varied and brilliant talent and of a generous and gallant spirit was asked at a dinner table, one evening not many years ago, why no women appeared in his stories. He promptly replied that he admired pluck above all other qualities, that he was timid by nature and had won courage at the point of danger, and cared for it as the most splendid of manly qualities. There happened to be a woman present who bore the name of one of the most daring men of the time, and who knew army life intimately. She made no comment and offered no objection to the implication of the eminent writer's incautious statement; but presently she began, in a very quiet tone, to describe the incidents of her experience in army posts and on the march, and every body listened intently as she went on narrating story after story of the pluck and indifference to danger of women on the frontier posts and, in some instances, on the march. The eminent writer remained silent, but the moment the woman withdrew from the table he was eager to know who the teller of these stories of heroism was and how she had happened upon such remarkable experiences; and it was noted that a woman appeared in his next novel!

The stories in this volume have been collected from many sources in the endeavour to illustrate the wide range of heroism in the lives of brave and noble women, and with the hope that these records of splendid or quiet courage will open the eyes of young readers to the many forms which heroism wears, and furnish a more spiritual scale of heroic qualities.

Hamilton W. Mabie.

I
ALCESTIS

Asclepius, the son of Apollo, being a mighty physician, raised men from the dead. But Zeus was wroth that a man should have such power, and so make of no effect the ordinance of the gods. Wherefore he smote Asclepius with a thunderbolt and slew him. And when Apollo knew this, he slew the Cyclopés that had made the thunderbolts for his father Zeus, for men say that they make them on their forges that are in the mountain of Etna.

Zeus suffered not this deed to go unpunished, but passed this sentence on his son Apollo, that he should serve a mortal man for the space of a whole year. Wherefore, for all that he was a god, he kept the sheep of Admetus, who was the Prince of Pheræ in Thessaly. And Admetus knew not that he was a god; but, nevertheless, being a just man, dealt truly with him.

And it came to pass after this that Admetus was sick unto death. But Apollo gained this grace for him of the Fates (who order of life and death for men), that he should live, if only he could find some one who should be willing to die in his stead. And he went to all his kinsmen and friends and asked this thing of them, but found no one that was willing so to die; only Alcestis his wife was willing.

And when the day was come on the which it was appointed for her to die, Death came that he might fetch her. And when he was come, he found Apollo walking to and for before the palace of King Admetus, having his bow in his hand. And when Death saw him, he said:

"What doest thou here, Apollo? Is it not enough for thee to have kept Admetus from his doom? Dost thou keep watch and ward over this woman with thine arrows and thy bow?"

"Fear not," the god made answer, "I have justice on my side."

"If thou hast justice, what need of thy bow?"

"'Tis my wont to carry it."

"Ay, and it is thy wont to help this house beyond all right and law."

"Nay, but I was troubled at the sorrows of one that I loved, and helped him."

"I know thy cunning speech and fair ways; but this woman thou shalt not take from me."

"But consider; thou canst have but one life. Wilt thou not take another in her stead?"

"Her and no other will I have, for my honour is the greater when I take the young."

"I know thy temper, hated both of gods and of men. But there cometh a guest to this house, whom Eurystheus sendeth to the snowy plains of Thrace, to fetch the horses of Diomed. Haply he shall persuade thee against thy will."

"Say what thou wilt; it shall avail nothing. And now I go to cut off a lock of her hair, for I take these first-fruits of them that die."

In the meantime, within the palace, Alcestis prepared herself for death. And first she washed her body with pure water from the river, and then she took from her coffer of cedar her fairest apparel, and adorned herself therewith. Then, being so arranged, she stood before the hearth and prayed, saying:

"O Queen Heré, behold! I depart this day. Do thou therefore keep my children, giving to this one a noble husband and to that a loving wife."

And all the altars that were in the house she visited in like manner, crowning them with myrtle leaves and praying at them. Nor did she weep at all, or groan, or grow pale. But at the last, when she came to her chamber, she cast herself upon the bed and kissed it, crying:

"I hate thee not, though I die for thee, giving myself for my husband. And thee another wife shall possess, not more true than I am, but, maybe, more fortunate!"

And after she had left the chamber, she turned to it again and again with many tears.

And all the while her children clung to her garments, and she took them up in her arms, the one first and then the other, and kissed them. And all the servants that were in the house bewailed their mistress, nor did she fail to reach her hand to each of them greeting him. There was not one of them so vile but she spake to him and was spoken to again.

After this, when the hour was now come when she must die, she cried to her husband (for he held her in his arms, as if he would have stayed her that she should not depart):

"I see the boat of the dead, and Charon standing with his hand upon the pole, who calleth me, saying, 'Hasten; thou delayest us'; and then again, 'A winged messenger of the dead looketh at me from under his dark eyebrows, and would lead me away. Dost thou not see him?'"

Then, after this, she seemed now ready to die, yet again she gathered strength, and said to the King:

"Listen, and I will tell thee before I die what I would have thee do. Thou knowest how I have given my life for thy life. For when I might have lived, and had for my husband any prince of Thessaly that I would, and dwelt here in wealth and royal state, yet could I not endure to be widowed of thee and that thy children should be fatherless. Therefore I spared not myself, though thy father and mother betrayed thee. But the gods have ordered all this after their own pleasure. So be it. Do thou therefore make this recompense, which indeed thou owest to me, for what will not a man give for his life? Thou lovest these children even as I love them. Suffer them then to be rulers in this house, and bring not a stepmother over them who shall hate them and deal with them unkindly. A son, indeed, hath a tower of strength in his father. But, O my daughter, how shall it fare with thee, for thy mother will not give thee in marriage, nor be with thee, comforting thee when a mother most showeth kindness and love. And now farewell, for I die this day. And thou, too, farewell, my husband. Thou losest a true wife, and ye, too, my children, a true mother."

Then Admetus made answer:

"Fear not, it shall be as thou wilt. I could not find other wife fair and well born and true as thou. Never more shall I gather revellers in my palace, or crown my head with garlands, or hearken to the voice of music. Never shall I touch the harp or sing to the Libyan flute. And some cunning craftsman shall make an image fashioned like unto thee, and this I will hold in my arms and think of thee. Cold comfort indeed, yet that shall ease somewhat of the burden of my soul. But oh! that I had the voice and melody of Orpheus, for then had I gone down to Hell and persuaded the Queen thereof or her husband with my song to let thee go; nor would the watch-dog of Pluto, nor Charon that ferrieth the dead, have hindered me but that I had brought thee to the light. But do thou wait for me there, for there will I dwell with thee; and when I die they shall lay me by thy side, for never was wife so true as thou."

Then said Alcestis:

"Take these children as a gift from me, and be as a mother to them."

"O me!" he cried, "what shall I do, being bereaved of thee?"

And she said:

"Time will comfort thee; the dead are as nothing."

But he said:

"Nay, but let me depart with thee."

But the Queen made answer:

"'Tis enough that I die in thy stead."

And when she had thus spoken she gave up the ghost.

Then the King said to the old men that were gathered together to comfort him:

"I will see to this burial. And do ye sing a hymn as is meet to the god of the dead. And to all my people I make this decree; that they mourn for this woman, and clothe themselves in black, and shave their heads, and that such as have horses cut off their manes, and that there be not heard in the city the voice of the flute or the sound of the harp for the space of twelve months."

Then the old men sang the hymn as they had been bidden. And when they had finished, it befell that Hercules, who was on a journey, came to the palace and asked whether King Admetus was sojourning there.

And the old men answered:

"'Tis even so, Hercules. But what, I pray thee, bringeth thee to this land?"

"I am bound on an errand for King Eurystheus; even to bring back to him horses of King Diomed."

"How wilt thou do this? Dost thou not know this Diomed?"

"I know naught of him, nor of his land."

"Thou wilt not master him or his horses without blows."

"Even so, yet I may not refuse the tasks that are set to me."

"Thou art resolved then to do this thing or to die?"

"Ay; and this is not the first race that I have run."

"Thou wilt not easily bridle these horses."

"Why not? They breathe not fire from their nostrils."

"No, but they devour the flesh of men."

"What sayest thou? This is the food of wild beasts, not of horses."

"Yet 'tis true. Thou wilt see their mangers foul with blood."

"And the master of these steeds, whose son is he?"

"He is son of Ares, lord of the land of Thrace."

"Now this is a strange fate and a hard that maketh me fight ever with the sons of Ares, with Lycaon first, and with Cycnus next, and now with this King Diomed. But none shall ever see the son of Alcmena trembling before an enemy."

And now King Admetus came forth from the palace. And when the two had greeted one another, Hercules would fain know why the King had shaven his hair as one that mourned for the dead. And the King answered that he was about to bury that day one that was dear to him.

And when Hercules inquired yet further who this might be, the King said that his children were well, and his father also, and his mother. But of his wife he answered so that Hercules understood not that he spake of her. For he said that she was a stranger by blood, yet near in friendship, and that she had dwelt in his house, having been left an orphan of her father.

Nevertheless Hercules would have departed and found entertainment elsewhere, for he would not be troublesome to his host. But the King suffered him not. And to the servant that stood by he said:

"Take thou this guest to the guest-chamber; and see that they that have charge of these matters set abundance of food before him. And take care that ye shut the doors between the chambers and the palace; for it is not meet that the guest at his meal should hear the cry of them that mourn."

And when the old men would know why the King, having so great a trouble upon him, yet entertained a guest, he made answer:

"Would ye have commended me the more if I had caused him to depart from this house and this city? For my sorrow had not been one whit the less, and I had lost the praise of hospitality. And a right worthy host is he to me if ever I chance to visit the land of Argos."

And now they had finished all things for the burying of Alcestis, when the old man Pheres, the father of the King, approached, and servants came with him bearing robes and crowns and other adornments wherewith to do honour to the dead. And when he was come over against the bier whereon they laid the dead woman, he spake to the King, saying:

"I am come to mourn with thee, my son, for thou hast lost a noble wife. Only thou must endure, though this indeed is a hard thing. But take these adornments, for it is meet that she should be honoured who died for thee, and for me also, that I should not go down to the grave childless." And to the dead he said, "Fare thee well, noble wife, that hast kept this house from falling. May it be well with thee in the dwellings of the dead!"

But the King answered him in great wrath:

"I did not bid thee to this burial, nor shall this dead woman be adorned with gifts of thine. Who art thou that thou shouldest bewail her? Surely thou art not father of mine. For being come to extreme old age, yet thou wouldst not die for thy son, but sufferedst this woman, being a stranger in blood, to die for me. Her, therefore, I count father and mother also. Yet this had been a noble deed for thee, seeing that the span of life that was left to thee was short. And I, too, had not been left to live out my days thus miserably, bereaved of her whom I loved. Hast thou not had all happiness, thus having lived in kingly power from youth to age? And thou wouldst have left a son to come after thee, that thy house should not be spoiled by thine enemies. Have I not always done due reverence to thee and to my mother? And, lo! this is the recompense that ye make me. Wherefore I say to thee, make haste and raise other sons who may nourish thee in thy old age, and pay thee due honour when thou art dead, for I will not bury thee. To thee I am dead."

Then the old man spake:

"Thinkest thou that thou art driving some Lydian and Phrygian slave that hath been bought with money, and forgettest that I am a freeborn man of Thessaly, as my father was freeborn before me? I reared thee to rule this house after me; but to die for thee, that I owed thee not. This is no custom among the Greeks that a father should die for his son. To thyself thou livest or diest. All that was thy due thou hast received of me; the kingdom over many people, and, in due time, broad lands which I also received of my father. How have I wronged thee? Of what have I defrauded thee? I ask thee not to die for me; and I die not for thee. Thou lovest to behold this light. Thinkest thou that thy father loveth it not? For the years of the dead are very long; but the days of the living are short yet sweet withal. But I say to thee that thou hast fled from thy fate in shameless fashion, and hast slain this woman. Yea, a woman hath vanquished thee, and yet thou chargest cowardice against me. In truth, 'tis a wise device of thine that thou mayest live forever, if marrying many times, thou canst still persuade thy wife to die for thee. Be silent, then, for shame's sake; and if thou lovest life, remember that others love it also."

So King Admetus and his father reproached each other with many unseemly words. And when the old man had departed, they carried forth Alcestis to her burial.

But when they that bare the body had departed, there came in the old man that had the charge of the guest-chambers, and spake, saying:

"I have seen many guests that have come from all the lands under the sun to this palace of Admetus, but never have I given entertainment to such evil guest as this. For first, knowing that my lord was in sore trouble and sorrow, he forebore not to enter these gates. And then he took his entertainment in most unseemly fashion; for if he lacked aught he would call loudly for it; and then, taking a great cup wreathed with leaves of ivy in his hands, he drank of red wine untempered with water. And when the food had warmed him, he crowned his head with myrtle boughs, and sang in the vilest fashion. Then might one hear two melodies, this fellow's songs, which he sang without thought for the troubles of my lord and the lamentation wherewith we servants lamented our mistress. But we suffered not this stranger to see our tears, for so my lord had commanded. Surely this is a grievous thing that I must entertain this stranger, who surely is some thief or robber. And meanwhile they have taken my mistress to her grave, and I followed not after her, nor reached my hand to her, that was as a mother to all that dwell in this place."

When the man had so spoken, Hercules came forth from the guest-chamber, crowned with myrtle, and his face flushed with wine. And he cried to the servant, saying:

"Ho, there! why lookest thou so solemn and full of care? Thou shouldst not scowl on thy guest after this fashion, being full of some sorrow that concerns thee not nearly. Come hither, and I will teach thee to be wiser. Knowest thou what manner of thing the life of a man is? I trow not. Hearken therefore. There is not a man who knoweth what a day may bring forth. Therefore I say to thee: Make glad thy heart; eat, drink, count the day that now is to be thine own, but all else to be doubtful. As for all other things, let them be, and hearken to my words. Put away this great grief that lieth upon thee, and enter into this chamber. Right soon shall I ease thee of these gloomy thoughts. As thou art a man, be wise after the fashion of a man; for to them that are of a gloomy countenance, life, if only I judge rightly, is not life but trouble only."

Then the servant answered:

"All this I know; but we have fared so ill in this house that mirth and laughter ill beseem us."

"But they tell me that this dead woman was a stranger. Why shouldst thou be so troubled, seeing that they who rule this house yet live?"

"How sayest thou that they live? Thou knowest not what trouble we endure."

"I know it, unless thy lord strangely deceived me."

"My lord is given to hospitality."

"And should it hinder him that there is some stranger dead in the house?"

"A stranger, sayest thou? 'Tis passing strange to call her thus."

"Hath thy lord then suffered some sorrow that he told thee not?"

"Even so, or I had not loathed to see thee at thy revels. Thou seest this shaven hair and these black robes."

"What then? Who is dead? One of thy lord's children, or the old man, his father?"

"Stranger, 'tis the wife of Admetus that is dead."

"What sayest thou? And yet he gave me entertainment?"

"Yea, for he would not, for shame, turn thee from his house."

"O miserable man, what a helpmeet thou hast lost!"

"Ay, and we are all lost with her."

"Well I knew it; for I saw the tears in his eyes, and his head shaven, and his sorrowful regard; but he deceived me, saying that the dead woman was a stranger. Therefore did I enter the doors and make merry, and crown myself with garlands, not knowing what had befallen my host. But, come, tell me; where doth he bury her? Where shall I find her?"

"Follow straight along the road that leadeth to Larissa, and thou shalt see her tomb in the outskirts of the city."

Then said Hercules to himself:

"O my heart, thou hast dared many great deeds before this day; and now most of all must I show myself a true son of Zeus. Now will I save this dead woman Alcestis, and give her back to her husband, and make due recompense to Admetus. I will go, therefore, and watch for this black-robed king, even Death. Methinks I shall find him nigh unto the tomb, drinking the blood of the sacrifices. There will I lie in wait for him, and run upon him, and throw my arms about him, nor shall anyone deliver him out of my hands, till he have given up to me this woman. But if it chance that I find him not there, and he come not to the feast of blood, I will go down to the Queen of Hell, to the land where the sun shineth not, and beg her of the Queen; and doubtless she will give her to me, that I may give her to her husband. Right nobly did he entertain me, and drave me not from his house, for all that he had been stricken by such sorrow. Is there a man in Thessaly, nay in the whole land of Greece, that is such a lover of hospitality? I trow not. Noble is he, and he shall know that he is no ill friend to whom he hath done this thing."

So Hercules went his way. And when he was gone Admetus came back from the burying of his wife, a great company following him, of whom the elders sought to comfort him in his sorrow. And when he was come to the gates of his palace he cried:

"How shall I enter thee? how shall I dwell in thee? Once I came within thy gates with many pine-torches from Pelion, and the merry noise of the marriage song, holding in my hand the hand of her that is dead; and after us followed a troop that magnified her and me, so noble a pair we were. And now with wailing instead of marriage songs, and garments of black for white wedding robes, I go to my desolate couch."

But while he yet lingered before the palace Hercules came back, leading with him a woman that was covered with a veil. And when he saw the King, he said:

"I hold it well to speak freely to one that is a friend, and that a man should not hide a grudge in his heart. Hear me, therefore. Though I was worthy to be counted thy friend, yet thou saidst not that thy wife lay dead in thy house, but suffered me to feast and make merry. For this, therefore, I blame thee. And now I will tell thee why I am returned. I pray thee, keep this woman against the day when I shall come back from the land of Thrace, bringing the horses of King Diomed. And if it should fare ill with me, let her abide here and serve thee. Not without toil came she into my hands. I found as I went upon my way that certain men had ordered contests for wrestlers and runners, and the like. Now for them that had the preëminence in lesser things there were horses for prizes; and for the greater, as wrestling and boxing, a reward of oxen, to which was added this woman. And now I would have thee keep her, for which thing, haply, thou wilt one day thank me."

To this the King answered:

"I thought no slight when I hid this truth from thee. Only it would have been for me sorrow upon sorrow if thou hadst gone to the house of another. But as for this woman, I would have thee ask this thing of some prince of Thessaly that hath not suffered such grief as I. In Pheræ here thou hast many friends; but I could not look upon her without tears. Add not then this new trouble. And also how could she, being young, abide in my house, for young I judge her to be? And of a truth, lady, thou art very like in shape and stature to my Alcestis that is dead. I pray you, take her from my sight, for she troubleth my heart, and my tears run over with beholding her."

Then said Hercules:

"Would I had such strength that I could bring back thy wife from the dwellings of the dead, and put her in thy hands."

"I know thy good will, but what profiteth it? No man may bring back the dead."

"Well, time will soften thy grief, which yet is new."

"Yea, if by time thou meanest death."

"But a new wife will comfort thee."

"Hold thy peace; such a thing cometh not into my thoughts."

"What? wilt thou always keep this widowed state?"

"Never shall woman more be wife of mine."

"What will this profit her that is dead?"

"I know not, yet had I sooner die than be false to her."

"Yet I would have thee take this woman into thy house."

"Ask it not of me, I entreat thee, by thy father Zeus."

"Thou wilt lose much if thou wilt not do it."

"And if I do it I shall break my heart."

"Haply some day thou wilt thank me; only be persuaded."

"Be it so; they shall take the woman into the house."

"I would not have thee entrust her to thy servants."

"If thou so thinkest, lead her in thyself."

"Nay, but I would give her into thy hands."

"I touch her not, but my house she may enter."

"'Tis only to thy hand I entrust her."

"O King, thou compellest me to this against my will."

"Stretch forth thy hand and touch her."

"I touch her as I would touch the Gorgon's head."

"Hast thou hold of her?"

"I have hold."

"Then keep her safe, and say that the son of Zeus is a noble friend. See if she be like thy wife; and change thy sorrow for joy."

And when the King looked, lo! the veiled woman was Alcestis his wife.

II

ANTIGONE

It befell in times past that the gods, being angry with the inhabitants of Thebes, sent into their land a very noisome beast which men called the Sphinx. Now this beast had the face and breast of a fair woman, but the feet and claws of a lion; and it was wont to ask a riddle of such as encountered it; and such as answered not aright it would tear and devour.

When it had laid waste the land many days, there chanced to come to Thebes one Œdipus, who had fled from the city of Corinth that he might escape the doom which the gods had spoken against him. And the men of the place told him of the Sphinx, how she cruelly devoured the people, and that he who should deliver them from her should have the kingdom. So Œdipus, being very bold, and also ready of wit, went forth to meet the monster. And when she saw him she spake, saying:

"Read me this riddle right, or die: What liveth there beneath the sky, Four-footed creature that doth choose Now three feet and now twain to use, And still more feebly o'er the plain Walketh with three feet than with twain?"

And Œdipus made reply:

"'Tis man, who in life's early day Four-footed crawleth on his way; When time hath made his strength complete, Upright his form and twain his feet; When age hath bowed him to the ground A third foot in his staff is found."

And when the Sphinx found that her riddle was answered, she cast herself from a high rock and perished.

For a while Œdipus reigned in great power and glory; but afterwards in madness he put out his own eyes. Then his two sons cast him into prison, and took his kingdom, making agreement between themselves that each should reign for the space of one year. And the elder of the two, whose name was Eteocles, first had the kingdom; but when his year was come to an end, he would not abide by his promise, but kept that which he should have given up, and drave out his younger brother from the city. Then the younger, whose name was Polynices, fled to Argos, to King Adrastus. And after a while he married the daughter of the King, who made a covenant with him that he would bring him back with a high hand to Thebes, and set him on the throne of his father. Then the King sent messengers to certain of the princes of Greece, entreating that they would help in this matter. And of these some would not, but others hearkened to his words, so that a great army was gathered together and followed the King and Polynices to make war against Thebes. So they came and pitched their camp over against the city. And after they had been there many days, the battle grew fierce about the wall. But the chiefest fight was between the two brothers, for the two came together in an open space before the gates. And first Polynices prayed to Heré, for she was the goddess of the great city of Argos, which had helped him in this enterprise, and Eteocles prayed to Pallas of the Golden Shield, whose temple stood hard by. Then they crouched, each covered with his shield, and holding his spear in his hand, if by chance his enemy should give occasion to smite him; and if one showed so much as an eye above the rim of his shield the other would strike at him. But after a while King Eteocles slipped upon a stone that was under his foot, and uncovered his leg, at which straightway Polynices took aim with his spear, piercing the skin. But so doing he laid his own shoulder bare, and King Eteocles gave him a wound in the breast. He brake his spear in striking, and would have fared ill but that with a great stone he smote the spear of Polynices, and brake this also in the middle. And now were the two equal, for each had lost his spear. So they drew their swords and came yet closer together. But Eteocles used a device which he had learnt in the land of Thessaly; for he drew his left foot back, as if he would have ceased from the battle, and then of a sudden moved the right forward; and so smiting sideways, drave his sword right through the body of Polynices. But when thinking that he had slain him he set his weapons in the earth, and began to spoil him of his arms, the other, for he yet breathed a little, laid his hand upon his sword, and though he had scarce strength to smite, yet gave the King a mortal blow, so that the two lay dead together on the plain. And the men of Thebes lifted up the bodies of the dead, and bare them both into the city.

When these two brothers, the sons of King Œdipus, had fallen each by the hand of the other, the kingdom fell to Creon their uncle. For not only was he the next of kin to the dead, but also the people held him in great honour because his son Menœceus had offered himself with a willing heart that he might deliver his city from captivity.

Now when Creon was come to the throne, he made a proclamation about the two princes, commanding that they should bury Eteocles with all honour, seeing that he died as beseemed a good man and a brave, doing battle for his country, that it should not be delivered into the hands of the enemy; but as for Polynices he bade them leave his body to be devoured by the fowls of the air and the beasts of the field, because he had joined himself to the enemy, and would have beaten down the walls of the city, and burned the temples of the gods with fire, and led the people captive. Also he commanded that if any man should break this decree he should suffer death by stoning.

Now Antigone, who was sister to the two princes, heard that the decree had gone forth, and chancing to meet her sister Ismené before the gates of the palace, spake to her, saying:

"O my sister, hast thou heard this decree that the King hath put forth concerning our brethren that are dead?"

Then Ismené made answer: "I have heard nothing my sister, only that we are bereaved of both of our brethren in one day, and that the army of the Argives is departed in this night that is now past. So much I know, but no more."

"Hearken then. King Creon hath made a proclamation that they shall bury Eteocles with all honour; but that Polynices shall lie unburied, that the birds of the air and the beasts of the field may devour him; and that whosoever shall break this decree shall suffer death by stoning."

"But if it be so, my sister, how can we avail to change it?"

"Think whether or no thou wilt share with me the doing of this deed."

"What deed? What meanest thou?"

"To pay due honour to this dead body."

"What? Wilt thou bury him when the King hath forbidden it?"

"Yea, for he is my brother and also thine, though, perchance, thou wouldst not have it so. And I will not play him false."

"O my sister, wilt thou do this when Creon hath forbidden it?"

"Why should he stand between me and mine?"

"But think now what sorrows are come upon our house. For our father perished miserably, having first put out his own eyes; and our mother hanged herself with her own hands; and our two brothers fell in one day, each by the other's spear; and now we two only are left. And shall we not fall into a worse destruction than any, if we transgress these commands of the King? Think, too, that we are women and not men, and of necessity obey them that are stronger. Wherefore, as for me, I will pray the dead to pardon me, seeing that I am thus constrained; but I will obey them that rule."

"I advise thee not, and, if thou thinkest thus, I would not have thee for helper. But know that I will bury my brother, nor could I better die than for doing such a deed. For as he loved me, so also do I love him greatly. And shall not I do pleasure to the dead rather than to the living, seeing that I shall abide with the dead for ever? But thou, if thou wilt, do dishonour to the laws of the gods?"

"I dishonour them not. Only I cannot set myself against the powers that be."

"So be it; but I will bury my brother."

"O my sister, how I fear for thee!"

"Fear for thyself. Thine own lot needeth all thy care."

"Thou wilt at least keep thy counsel, nor tell the thing to any man."

"Not so: hide it not. I shall scorn thee more if thou proclaim it not aloud to all."

So Antigone departed; and after a while came to the same place King Creon, clad in his royal robes, and with his sceptre in his hand, and set forth his counsel to the elders who were assembled, how he had dealt with the two princes according to their deserving, giving all honour to him that loved his country and casting forth the other unburied. And he bade them take care that this decree should be kept, saying that he had also appointed certain men to watch the dead body.

But he had scarcely left speaking when there came one of these same watchers and said:

"I have not come hither in haste, O King, nay, I doubted much, while I was yet on the way, whether I should not turn again. For now I thought, 'Fool, why goest thou where thou shalt suffer for it'; and then, again, 'Fool, the King will hear the matter elsewhere, and then how wilt thou fare?' But at the last I came as I had purposed, for I know that nothing may happen to me contrary to fate."

"But say," said the King, "what troubles thee so much?"

"First hear my case. I did not the thing, and know not who did it, and it were a grievous wrong should I fall into trouble for such a cause."

"Thou makest a long preface, excusing thyself, but yet hast, as I judge, something to tell."

"Fear, my lord, ever causeth delay."

"Wilt thou not speak out thy news and then begone?"

"I will speak it. Know then that some man hath thrown dust upon this dead corpse, and done besides such things as are needful."

"What sayest thou? Who hath dared to do this deed?"

"That I know not, for there was no mark as of spade or pick-axe; nor was the earth broken, nor had wagon passed thereon. We were sore dismayed when the watchman showed the thing to us; for the body we could not see. Buried indeed it was not, but rather covered with dust. Nor was there any sign as of wild beast or of dog that had torn it. Then there arose a contention among us, each blaming the other, and accusing his fellows, and himself denying that he had done the deed or was privy to it. And doubtless we had fallen to blows but that one spake a word which made us all tremble for fear, knowing that it must be as he said. For he said that the thing must be told to thee, and in no wise hidden. So we drew lots, and by evil chance the lot fell upon me. Wherefore I am here, not willingly, for no man loveth him that bringing evil tidings."

Then said the chief of the old men:

"Consider, O King, for haply this thing is from the gods."

But the King cried:

"Thinkest thou that the gods care for such an one as this dead man, who would have burnt their temples with fire, and laid waste the land which they love, and set at naught the laws? Not so. But there are men in this city who have long time had ill will to me, not bowing their necks to my yoke; and they have persuaded these fellows with money to do this thing. Surely there never was so evil a thing as money, which maketh cities into ruinous heaps, and banisheth men from their houses, and turneth their thoughts from good unto evil. But as for them that have done this deed for hire, of a truth they shall not escape, for I say to thee, fellow, if ye bring not here before my eyes the man that did this thing, I will hang you up alive. So shall ye learn that ill gains bring no profit to a man."

So the guard departed; but as he went he said to himself:

"Now may the gods grant that the man be found; but however this may be, thou shalt not see me come again on such errand as this, for even now have I escaped beyond all hope."

Notwithstanding, after a space he came back with one of his fellows; and they brought with them the maiden Antigone, with her hands bound together.

And it chanced that at the same time King Creon came forth from the palace. Then the guard set forth the thing to him, saying:

"We cleared away the dust from the dead body, and sat watching it. And when it was now noon, and the sun was at his height, there came a whirlwind over the plain, driving a great cloud of dust. And when this had passed, we looked, and lo! this maiden whom we have brought hither stood by the dead corpse. And when she saw that it lay bare as before, she sent up an exceeding bitter cry, even as a bird whose young ones have been taken from the nest. Then she cursed them that had done this deed; and brought dust and sprinkled it upon the dead man, and poured water upon him three times. Then we ran and laid hold upon her, and accused her that she had done this deed; and she denied it not. But as for me, 'tis well to have escaped from death, but it is ill to bring friends into the same. Yet I hold that there is nothing dearer to a man than his life."

Then said the King to Antigone:

"Tell me in a word, didst thou know my decree?"

"I knew it. Was it not plainly declared?"

"How daredst thou to transgress the laws?"

"Zeus made not such laws, nor Justice that dwelleth with the gods below. I judged not that thy decrees had such authority that a man should transgress for them the unwritten sure commandments of the gods. For these, indeed, are not of to-day or yesterday, but they live for ever, and their beginning no man knoweth. Should I, for fear of thee, be found guilty against them? That I should die I knew. Why not? All men must die. And if I die before my time, what loss? He who liveth among many sorrows even as I have lived, counteth it gain to die. But had I left my own mother's son unburied, this had been loss indeed."

Then said the King:

"Such stubborn thoughts have a speedy fall, and are shivered even as the iron that hath been made hard in the furnace. And as for this woman and her sister—for I judge her sister to have had a part in this matter—though they were nearer to me than all my kindred, yet shall they not escape the doom of death. Wherefore let some one bring the other woman hither."

And while they went to fetch the maiden Ismené, Antigone said to the King:

"Is it not enough for thee to slay me? What need to say more? For thy words please me not nor mine thee. Yet what nobler thing could I have done than to bury my mother's son? And so would all men say but fear shutteth their mouths."

"Nay," said the King, "none of the children of Cadmus thinketh thus, but thou only. But, hold, was not he that fell in battle with this man thy brother also?"

"Yes, truly, my brother he was."

"And dost thou not dishonour him when thou honourest his enemy?"

"The dead man would not say it, could he speak."

"Shall then the wicked have like honour with the good?"

"How knowest thou but that such honour pleaseth the gods below?"

"I have no love for them I hate, though they be dead."

"Of hating I know nothing: 'tis enough for me to love."

"If thou wilt love, go love the dead. But while I live no woman shall rule me."

Then those that had been sent to fetch the maiden Ismené brought her forth from the palace. And when the King accused her that she had been privy to the deed she denied not, but would have shared one lot with her sister.

But Antigone turned from her, saying:

"Not so; thou hast no part or lot in the matter. For thou hast chosen life, and I have chosen death; and even so shall it be."

And when Ismené saw that she prevailed nothing with her sister, she turned to the King and said:

"Wilt thou slay the bride of thy son?"

"Ay," said he, "there are other brides to win!"

"But none," she made reply, "that accord so well with him."

"I will have no evil wives for my sons," said the King.

Then cried Antigone:

"O Hæmon, whom I love, how thy father wrongeth thee!"

Then the King bade the guards lead the two into the palace. But scarcely had they gone when there came to the place the Prince Hæmon, the King's son, who was betrothed to the maiden Antigone. And when the King saw him, he said:

"Art thou content, my son, with thy father's judgment?"

And the young man answered:

"My father, I would follow thy counsels in all things."

Then said the King:

"'Tis well spoken, my son. This is a thing to be desired, that a man should have obedient children. But if it be otherwise with a man, he hath gotten great trouble for himself, and maketh sport for them that hate him. And now as to this matter. There is naught worse than an evil wife. Wherefore I say let this damsel wed a bridegroom among the dead. For since I have found her, alone of all this people, breaking my decree, surely she shall die. Nor shall it profit her to claim kinship with me, for he that would rule a city must first deal justly with his own kindred. And as for obedience, this it is that maketh a city to stand both in peace and in war."

To this the Prince Hæmon made answer:

"What thou sayest, my father, I do not judge. Yet bethink thee, that I see and hear on thy behalf what is hidden from thee. For common men cannot abide thy look if they say that which pleaseth thee not. Yet do I hear it in secret. Know then that all the city mourneth for this maiden, saying that she dieth wrongfully for a very noble deed, in that she buried her brother. And 'tis well, my father, not to be wholly set on thy thoughts, but to listen to the counsels of others."

"Nay," said the King; "shall I be taught by such an one as thou?"

"I pray thee regard my words, if they be well, and not my years."

"Can it be well to honour them that transgress? And hath not this woman transgressed?"

"The people of this city judgeth not so."

"The people, sayest thou? Is it for them to rule, or for me?"

"No city is the possession of one man only."

So the two answered one the other, and their anger waxed hot. And at the last the King cried:

"Bring this accursed woman, and slay her before his eyes."

And the Prince answered:

"That thou shalt never do. And know this also, that thou shalt never see my face again."

So he went away in a rage; and the old men would have appeased the King's wrath, but he would not hearken to them, but said that the two maidens should die.

"Wilt thou then slay them both?" said the old men.

"'Tis well said," the King made answer. "Her that meddled not with the matter I harm not."

"And how wilt thou deal with the other?"

"There is a desolate place, and there I will shut her up alive in a sepulchre; yet giving her so much of food as shall quit us of guilt in the matter, for I would not have the city defiled. There let her persuade Death whom she loveth so much, that he harm her not."

So the guards led Antigone away to shut her up alive in the sepulchre. But scarcely had they departed when there came an old prophet Tiresias, seeking the King. Blind he was, so that a boy led him by the hand; but the gods had given him to see things to come.

And when the King saw him he asked:

"What seekest thou, wisest of men?"

Then the prophet answered:

"Hearken, O King, and I will tell thee. I sat in my seat, after my custom, in the place whither all manner of birds resort. And as I sat I heard a cry of birds that I knew not, very strange and full of wrath. And I knew that they tare and slew each other, for I heard the fierce flapping of their wings. And being afraid, I made inquiry about the fire, how it burned upon the altars. And this boy, for as I am a guide to others so he guideth me, told me that it shone not at all, but smouldered and was dull, and that the flesh which was burnt upon the altar spluttered in the flame, and wasted away into corruption and filthiness. And now I tell thee, O King, that the city is troubled by thy ill counsels. For the dogs and the birds of the air tear the flesh of this dead son of Œdipus, whom thou sufferest not to have due burial, and carry it to the altars, polluting them therewith. Wherefore the gods receive not from us prayer or sacrifice; and the cry of the birds hath an evil sound, for they are full of the flesh of a man. Therefore I bid thee be wise in time. For all men may err; but he that keepeth not his folly, but repenteth, doeth well; but stubbornness cometh to great trouble."

Then the King answered:

"Old man, I know the race of prophets full well, how ye sell your art for gold. But, make thy trade as thou wilt, this man shall not have burial; yea, though the eagles of Zeus carry his flesh to their master's throne in heaven, he shall not have it."

And when the prophet spake again, entreating him, and warning, the King answered him after the same fashion, that he spake not honestly, but had sold his art for money.

But at the last the prophet spake in great wrath, saying:

"Know, O King, that before many days shall pass, thou shalt pay a life for a life, even one of thine own children, for them with whom thou hast dealt unrighteously, shutting up the living with the dead, and keeping the dead from them to whom they belong. Therefore the Furies lie in wait for thee, and thou shalt see whether or no I speak these things for money. For there shall be mourning and lamentation in thine own house; and against thy people shall be stirred up many cities. And now, my child, lead me home, and let this man rage against them that are younger than I."

So the prophet departed, and the old men were sore afraid, and said:

"He hath spoken terrible things, O King; nor ever since these gray hairs were black have we known him say that which was false."

"Even so," said the King, "and I am troubled in heart, and yet am loath to depart from my purpose."

"King Creon," said the old men, "thou needest good counsel."

"What, then, would ye have done?"

"Set free the maiden from the sepulchre, and give this dead man burial."

Then the King cried to his people that they should bring bars wherewith to loosen the doors of the sepulchre, and hastened with them to the place. But coming on their way to the body of Prince Polynices, they took it up, and washed it, and buried that which remained of it, and raised over the ashes a great mound of earth. And this being done, they drew near to the place of the sepulchre; and as they approached, the King heard within a very piteous voice, and knew it for the voice of his son. Then he bade his attendants loose the door with all speed; and when they had loosed it, they beheld within a very piteous sight. For the maiden Antigone had hanged herself by the girdle of linen which she wore, and the young man Prince Hæmon stood with his arms about her dead body, embracing it. And when the King saw him, he cried to him to come forth; but the Prince glared fiercely upon him and answered him not a word, but drew his two-edged sword. Then the King, thinking that his son was minded in his madness to slay him, leapt back, but the Prince drave the sword into his own heart, and fell forward on the earth, still holding the dead maiden in his arms. And when they brought the tidings of these things to Queen Eurydice, the wife of King Creon and mother to the Prince, she could not endure the grief, being thus bereaved of her children, but laid hold of a sword, and slew herself therewith.

So the house of King Creon was left desolate unto him that day, because he despised the ordinances of the gods.

III

IPHIGENIA

King Agamemnon sat in his tent at Aulis, where the army of the Greeks was gathered together, being about to sail against the great city of Troy. It was now past midnight. But the King slept not, for he was careful and troubled about many things. And he had a lamp before him, and in his hand a tablet of pine wood, whereon he wrote. But he seemed not to remain in the same mind about that which he wrote; for now he would blot out the letters, and then would write them again; and now he fastened the seal upon the tablet and then brake it. And as he did this he wept, and was like to a man distracted. But after a while he called to an old man, his attendant (the man had been given in time past by Tyndareus to his daughter, Queen Clytæmnestra), and said:

"Old man, thou knowest how Galchas the soothsayer bade me offer for a sacrifice to Artemis, who is goddess of this place, my daughter Iphigenia, saying that so only should the army have a prosperous voyage from this place to Troy, and should take the city and destroy it; and how when I heard these words I bade Talthybius the herald go throughout the army and bid them depart, every man to his own country, for that I would not do this thing; and how my brother, King Menelaus, persuaded me so that I consented to it. Now, therefore, hearken to this, for what I am about to tell thee three men only know, namely, Calchas, the soothsayer, and Menelaus, and Ulysses, King of Ithaca. I wrote a letter to my wife the Queen, that she should send her daughter to this place, that she might be married to King Achilles; and I magnified the man to her, saying that he would in no wise sail with us unless I would give him my daughter in marriage. But now I have changed my purpose, and have written another letter after this fashion, as I will now set forth to thee: 'Daughter of Leda, send not thy child to the land of Eubœa, for I will Give Her in Marriage At Another Time.'"

"Ay," said the old man, "but how wilt thou deal with King Achilles? Will he not be wroth, hearing that he hath been cheated of his wife?"

"Not so," answered the King, "for we have indeed used his name, but he knoweth nothing of this marriage. And now make haste. Sit not thou down by any fountain in the woods, and suffer not thine eyes to sleep. And beware lest the chariot bearing the Queen and her daughter pass thee where the roads divide. And see that thou keep the seal upon this letter unbroken."

So the old man departed with the letter. But scarcely had he left the tent when King Menelaus spied him and laid hands on him, taking the letter and breaking the seal. And the old man cried out:

"Help, my lord; here is one hath taken thy letter!"

Then King Agamemnon came forth from his tent, saying:

"What meaneth this uproar and disputing that I hear?"

But even as he spake there came a messenger, saying:

"King Agamemnon, I am come, as thou badest me, with thy daughter Iphigenia. Also her mother, Queen Clytæmnestra, is come, bringing with her her little son, Orestes. And now they are resting themselves and their horses by the side of a spring, for indeed the way is long and weary. And all the army is gathered about them. And men question much wherefore they are come, saying, 'Doth the King make a marriage for his daughter; or hath he sent for her, desiring to see her?'"

King Agamemnon was sore dismayed when he knew that the Queen was come, and spake to himself:

"Now what shall I say to my wife? For that she is rightly come to the marriage of her daughter who can deny? But what will she say when she knoweth my purpose? And of the maiden, what shall I say? Unhappy maiden whose bridegroom shall be Death! For she will cry to me, 'Wilt thou kill me, my father?' And the little Orestes will wail, not knowing what he doeth, seeing he is but a babe."

And now King Menelaus came, saying that he repented, "For why should thy child die for me? What hath she to do with war? Let the army be scattered, so that wrong be not done."

Then said King Agamemnon:

"But how shall I escape from this strait? For the whole host will compel me to this deed?"

"Not so," said King Menelaus, "if thou wilt send back the maiden to Argos."

"But what shall that profit," said the King; "for Calchas will cause the matter to be known; or Ulysses, saying that I have failed of my promise; and if I fly to Argos, they will come and destroy my city and lay waste my land. Woe is me! in what a strait am I set! But take care, my brother, that Clytæmnestra hear nothing of these things."

When he had ended speaking, the Queen herself came unto the tent, riding in a chariot, having her daughter by her side. And she bade one of the attendants take out with care the caskets which she had brought for her daughter and bade others help her daughter to alight, and herself also, and to a fourth she said that he should take the young Orestes. Then Iphigenia greeted her father, saying:

"Thou hast done well to send for me, my father."

"'Tis true and yet not true, my child."

"Thou lookest not well pleased to see me, my father."

"He that is a king and commandeth a host hath many cares."

"Put away thy cares awhile, and give thyself to me."

"I am glad beyond measure to see thee."

"Glad art thou? Then why dost thou weep?"

"I weep because thou must be long time absent from me."

"Perish all these fightings and troubles!"

"They will cause many to perish, and me most miserably of all."

"Art thou going a journey from me, my father?"

"Ay, and thou also hast a journey to make."

"Must I make it alone, or with my mother?"

"Alone; neither father nor mother may be with thee."

"Sendest thou me to dwell elsewhere?"

"Hold thy peace: such things are not for maidens to inquire."

"Well, my father, order matters with the Phrygians, and then make haste to return."

"I must first make a sacrifice to the gods."

"'Tis well. The gods should have due honour."

"Ay, and thou wilt stand close to the altar."

"Shall I lead the dances, my father?"

"O my child, how I envy thee, that thou knowest naught! And now go into the tent; but first kiss me, and give me thy hand, for thou shalt be parted from thy father for many days."

And when she was gone within, he cried:

"O fair bosom and very lovely cheeks and yellow hair of my child! O city of Priam, what woe thou bringest on me! But I must say no more."

Then he turned to the Queen, and excused himself that he wept when he should rather have rejoiced for the marriage of his daughter. And when the Queen would know of the estate of the bridegroom, he told her that his name was Achilles, and that he was the son of Peleus and Thetis, daughter of Nereus of the sea, and that he dwelt in Phthia. And when she inquired of the time of the marriage, he said that it should be in the same moon, on the first lucky day; and as to the place, that it must be where the bridegroom was sojourning, that is to say, in the camp. "And I," said the King, "will give the maiden to her husband."

"But where," answered the Queen, "is it your pleasure that I should be?"

"Thou must return to Argos, and care for the maidens there."

"Sayest thou that I return? Who then will hold up the torch for the bride?"

"I will do that which is needful. For it is not seemly that thou shouldst be present where the whole army is gathered together."

"Ay, but it is seemly that a mother should give her daughter in marriage."

"But the maidens at home should not be left alone."

"They are well kept."

"Be persuaded, lady."

"Not so; thou shalt order that which is without the house, but I that which is within."

But now came Achilles, to tell the King that the army was growing impatient, saying, that unless they might sail speedily, they would return each man to his home. And when the Queen heard his name—for he had said to the attendant, "Tell thy master that Achilles, the son of Peleus, would speak with him"— she came forth from the tent and greeted him, and bade him give her his right hand. And when the young man was abashed she said:

"But why art thou abashed, seeing that thou art about to marry my daughter?"

And he answered:

"What sayest thou, lady? I cannot speak for wonder at thy words."

"Often men are ashamed when they see new friends, and the talk is of marriage."

"But lady, I never was suitor for thy daughter. Nor have the sons of Atreus said aught to me of the matter."

The Queen was beyond measure astonished, and cried:

"Now this is shameful indeed, that I should seek a bridegroom for my daughter in such fashion."

But when Achilles would have departed, to inquire of the King what this thing might mean, the old man that had at the first carried the letter came forth, and bade him stay. And when he had assurance that he would receive no harm for what he should tell them, he unfolded the whole matter. And when the Queen had heard it, she cried to Achilles:

"O son of Thetis of the sea! help me now in this strait, and help this maiden that hath been called thy bride! 'Twill be a shame to thee if such wrong be done under thy name; for it is thy name that hath undone us. Nor have I any altar to which I may flee, nor any friend but thee only in this army."

Then Achilles made answer:

"Lady, I learnt from the most righteous of men to be true and honest. Know, then, that thy daughter, seeing that she hath been given, though but in word only, to me, shall not be slain by her father. For if she so die, then shall my name be brought to great dishonour, since through it thou hast been persuaded to come with her to this place. This sword shall see right soon whether anyone will dare to take this maiden from me."

And now King Agamemnon came forth, saying that all things were ready for the marriage, and that they waited for the maiden.

"Tell me," cried the Queen, "dost thou purpose to slay thy daughter and mine?" And when he was silent, not knowing, indeed, what to say, she reproached him with many words, that she had been a loving and faithful wife to him, for which he made an ill recompense slaying her child.

And when she had made an end of speaking, the maiden came forth from the tent, holding the young child Orestes in her arms, and cast herself upon her knees before her father, and besought him, saying:

"I would, my father, that I had the voice of Orpheus, who made even the rocks to follow him, that I might persuade thee; but now all that I have I give, even these tears. O my father, I am thy child; slay me not before my time. This light is sweet to look upon. Drive me not from it to the land of darkness. I was the first to call thee father; and the first to whom thou didst say 'my child.' And thou wouldst say to me, 'Some day, my child, I shall see thee a happy wife in the home of a husband.' And I would answer, 'And I will receive thee with all love when thou art old, and pay thee back for all the benefits thou hast done unto me.' This I indeed remember, but thou forgettest; for thou art ready to slay me. Do it not, I beseech thee, by Pelops thy grandsire, and Atreus thy father, and this my mother. And thou, O my brother, though thou art but a babe, help me. Weep with me; beseech thy father that he slay not thy sister. O my father, though he be silent, yet, indeed, he beseecheth thee. For his sake, therefore, yea, and for mine own, have pity upon me, and slay me not."

But the King was sore distracted, knowing not what he should say or do, for a terrible necessity was upon him, seeing that the army could not make their journey to Troy unless this deed should first be done. And while he doubted came Achilles, saying that there was a horrible tumult in the camp, the men crying out that the maiden must be sacrificed, and that when he would have stayed them from their purpose, the people had stoned him with stones. Nevertheless, he said that he would fight for the maiden, even to the utmost; and that there were faithful men who would stand with and help him. But when the maiden heard these words, she stood forth and said:

"Hearken, my mother. Be not wroth with my father, for we cannot fight against Fate. Also we must take thought that this young man suffer not, for his help will avail naught, and he himself will perish. Therefore I am resolved to die. All Greece looketh to me. Without me the ships cannot make their voyage, nor the city of Troy be taken. Wherefore I will give myself for the people. Offer me for an offering; and let the Greeks take the city of Troy, for this shall be my memorial for ever."

Then said Achilles:

"Lady, I should count myself most happy if the gods would grant thee to be my wife. For I love thee well, when I see thee how noble thou art. And if thou wilt, I will carry thee to my home. And I doubt not that I shall save thee, though all the men of Greece be against me."

But the maiden answered:

"What I say, I say with full purpose. Nor will I that any man should die for me, but rather will I save this land of Greece."

And Achilles said:

"If this be thy will, lady, I cannot say nay. It is a noble thing that thou doest."

Nor was the maiden turned from her purpose though her mother besought her with many tears. So they that were appointed led her to the grove of Artemis, where there was built an altar, and the whole army of the Greeks gathered about. When the King saw her going to her death he covered his face with his mantle; but she stood by him, and said:

"I give my body with a willing heart to die for my country and for the whole land of Greece. I pray the gods that ye may prosper, and win the victory in this war, and come back safe to your homes. And now let no man touch me, for I will offer my neck to the sword with a good heart."

And all men marvelled to see the maiden of what a good courage she was. Then the herald Talthybius stood in the midst and commanded silence to the people; and Calchas the soothsayer put a garland about her head, and drew a sharp knife from his sheath. And all the army stood regarding the maiden and the priest and the altar.

Then there befell a marvellous thing. Calchas struck with his knife, for the sound of the stroke all men heard, but the maiden was not there. Whither she had gone no one knew; but in her stead there lay a great hind, and all the altar was red with the blood thereof.

And Calchas said:

"See ye this, men of Greece, how the goddess hath provided this offering in the place of the maiden, for she would not that her altar should be defiled with innocent blood. Be of good courage, therefore, and depart every man to his ship, for this day ye shall sail across the sea to the land of Troy."

IV

PAULA

In the city of Rome when its imperial strength had faded, to seek pleasure and to give one's self to display had taken the place of honest work and sober duty. The time of which we speak was the fourth century. Affairs of government had been moved to Constantinople, and the effects of the conduct of great matters in their midst was thus denied the Romans.

The populace, fed for ages on public doles and the terrible gaiety of gladiatorial shows had become thoroughly debased, and unable to work out their own bettering. The persons having riches were likewise degraded by a life of luxury and senseless extravagance. Men of that type aired themselves in lofty chariots, lazily reclining and showing to advantage their carefully curled hair, robes of silk embroidery and tissue of gold, to excite the admiration and envy of plainer livers. Their horses' harness would be covered with ornaments of gold, their coachmen armed with a golden wand instead of whip, and troups of slaves, parasites and other servitors would dance attendance about them. With such display the poor rich creatures would pass through the streets, pushing out of the way or trampling and crushing to the dust whomsoever they might chance to meet—very much as some automobilists act to-day. Brutality and senseless show always are hand in glove with each other.

The rich women of Rome well matched such men. Their very shoes crackled under their feet from excess of gold and silver ornament. Their dresses of cloth-of-gold or other expensive stuff were so heavy that the wearers could hardly walk, even with the aid of attendants. Their faces were often painted and their hair dyed and mounted high on the head in monstrous shapes and designs.

Creeping into such a life as we have just been describing came the pure and simple precepts of Jesus—and they doubtless found many a soul athirst and sick with folly and coarse regard for riches. For years the Christians had been persecuted and many of their number gaining the strength that poverty and persecution bring. In opposition to the luxury-loving spirit, also, had risen among a number an austere denial of all pleasure, and such persons sought a solitary life in a cave or other retired spot. The deserts were mined with caverns and holes in the sand in which hermits dwelt, picking up food as best they might, their bones rattling in a skin blackened by exposure—they were starving, praying and agonising for the salvation of their own souls and for a world sunk in luxury and wickedness.

Now and then one of these hermits would leave his country solitariness and go to some city with a mission of converting vice to virtue. Among these was a man whom we know as Jerome, or Saint Jerome. He was a native of a village on the slope of the Illyrian Alps, and his full name was Eusebius Hieronymus. Inflamed with a zeal for doing great works, loving controversy and harsh and strong in conflict, Jerome sought Rome after years of study and prayer in the desert. In Rome he came to be a frequenter of a palace on the Aventine in which a number of rich and influential women held meetings for Christian teaching and sought a truer and purer life.

Of all these women we best know Paula. No fine lady of that day was more exquisite, more fastidious, more splendid than she. She could not walk abroad without the support of servants, nor cross the marble floor from one silken couch to another, so heavily was gold interwoven in the tissue of her dresses. Her eldest daughter, Blæsilla, a widow at twenty, was a Roman exquisite, loving everything soft and luxurious. It was said of her that she spent entire days before her mirror giving herself to personal decoration—to the tower of curls on her head and the touch of rouge on her cheeks. Paula's second daughter, Paulina, had married a young patrician who was Christian.

The third member of the family, a girl of sixteen, was Eustochium, a character strongly contrasting with her beautiful mother and sister. Even in early years she had fixed her choice upon a secluded life and shown herself untouched by the gaudy luxury about her. And to this the following pretty story will bear witness. An aunt of hers was Prætextata, wife of a high official of the Emperor Julian, and like the Emperor a follower of the old faith in the gods rather than the new faith in the teachings of Jesus. The family of Paula were, however, as we said, Christian.

This aunt Prætextata saw with some impatience and anger what she considered the artificial gravity of her youthful niece, and when she heard that the maid had said she intended never to marry, and purposed to withdraw from the world, she invited Eustochium to her house on a visit. The young vestal donned her brown gown, the habit of humility, and all unsuspicious sought her aunt. She had scarcely found herself within the house, however, before she was seized by favourite maids, who were interested in the plot. They loosed Eustochium's long hair and elaborated it in curls and plaits; they took away her little brown gown and covered her with silk and cloth-of-gold; they hung upon her precious ornaments, and finally led her to the mirror to dazzle her eyes with the reflection she would find in the polished surface.

The little maid with the Greek name and pure heart, let them turn her round and round and praise her fresh and youthful beauty. But she was a girl who knew her mind, and was blessed with a natural seriousness. Her aunt's household she permitted to have their pleasure that day. Then again she donned her little brown gown; and wore the habit all her life.

To return to Jerome: he had hardly arrived in Rome when he was made secretary of a council held in that city by ecclesiastics in the year 382. During his stay he dwelt in the house upon the Aventine in which such women as Paula had been meeting. The little community were now giving up their excessive luxuries and were devoting their time and income to good works, to visiting the poor, tending the sick and founding the first hospitals. To the man of the desert the gentle life must have been more agreeable. In this retreat he accomplished the first portion of his great work, the first authoritative translation of the entire Canon of

Scripture—the Vulgate—so named when the Latin of Jerome was the language of the crowd.

But he did not work alone. Paula and other women of the community helped in the translation. They studied with enthusiasm the Scriptures in Hebrew and in Greek; they discussed phrases difficult of understanding, and often held their own opinions against the learned Jerome whose scribes they were willing to be.

Thus began the friendship between Paula and Jerome, which was deepened by the death of Blæsilla. This eldest daughter of Paula had a serious illness. One night, in a dream or vision, Jesus seemed to appear to her and take her by the hand and say, "Arise, come forth." Waking, she seemed to sit at the table like Mary of Bethany. From that night her whole life was changed. She gathered together her embroidered robes and her jewels and sold them for the poor. Instead of torturing her head with a mitre of curls, she wore a simple veil. A woollen cord, dark linen gown and common shoes replaced the gold embroidered girdle, the glistening silks and the golden-heeled shoes. She slept upon a hard couch. Like others of her family she was finely intelligent, and she became one of the "apprentices" of Jerome, who wrote for her a commentary on the book of Ecclesiastes, "Vanity of Vanities."

Her conversion was enduring, but her health failed. In a few months another attack of fever laid her low. Her funeral was magnificent. Paula, according to Roman custom, accompanied her child's body to the tomb of her ancestors, wild with grief, lamenting, and, at last, fainting, so that she was borne away as one dead.

The people were enraged. They accused Jerome, and other "detestable monks" of killing the young widow with austerities. "Let them," they said; "be stoned and thrown into the Tiber."

For days Paula wept and refused to see her friends. Jerome, because he had understood, loved and reverenced her child, she consented to admit. Paula listened to his telling her that she "refused nourishment not from love of fasting, but from love of sorrow"; that "the spirit of God descends only upon the humble," and she arose and went forth. Nothing ever interrupted the friendship which from that time made the joy of her life and of Jerome's.

It was in the summer of 385, nearly three years after his coming to Rome, and not a year after the death of Blæsilla, that Jerome left "Babylon," as he called the tumultuous city. An affectionate company followed him to the seaport. Soon after Paula prepared for her departure, dividing her patrimony among her children. Her daughter, Paulina, was now married to a good and faithful husband, and these two undertook the charge and rearing of their youngest sister and the little Toxotius, a boy of ten. The grave young Eustochium, her head now covered by the veil of the devotee, clung to her mother's side, a serene figure in the midst of all the misunderstanding and agitation of the parting.

Friends poured forth from the city to accompany them to the port, and all the way along the winding banks of the Tiber they plied Paula with entreaties and reproaches and tears. She made no answer. She was at all times slow to speak, the chronicle tells us. She freighted a ship at the port, Ostia, and retained her self-command until the vessel began to move from the shore where stood her son Toxotius stretching out his hands to her in last appeal, and by his side his sister Rufina, with wistful eyes. Paula's heart was like to burst. She turned her eyes away, unable to bear the sight, and would have fallen but for the support of the firm Eustochium standing by her mother's side.

The rich Roman lady, luxury-loving, had become a pilgrim. She had, however, according to the interpretation of the Christian spirit of that day, in renouncing her former life and all its belongings, set aside natural ties. Now she was going forth to make herself a home in the solitude of Bethlehem.

Her ship was occupied by her own party alone, and carried much baggage for this emigration for life. It came, hindered by no storms, to Cyprus, where old friends received Paula with honour, and conducted her to visit monks and nuns in their new establishments. She afterward proceeded to Antioch, where

Jerome joined the party, and then along the coast of Tyre and Sidon, by Herod's splendid city of Cæsarea and by Joppa rich with memories of the early apostles of their faith. Paula, the pilgrim, was no longer a tottering fine lady, but a strong, animated, interested traveller.

The little company continued on their tour for a year. They first paused, at Jerusalem, and here the tender, enthusiasm of Paula found its fullest expression. She went in a rapture of tears and exaltation from one to another of the sacred sites. She kissed the broken stone which was supposed to have been that rolled against the door of the Holy Sepulchre, and trod with pious awe the path to the cave where the True Cross was found. The legend of Helena's finding the cross was still fresh in those days, and doubts there were none.

The ecstasies and joy of Paula, which found their expression in rapturous prayers and tears, moved all Jerusalem. The city was thronged with pilgrims, and the great Roman lady became their wonder. The crowd followed her from point to point, marvelling at her frank emotion and the warmth of her natural feeling.

From Jerusalem the party set out to journey through the storied deserts of Syria. This was in the year 387. They stopped everywhere to visit those monasteries built in awful passes of the rocks and upon stony wastes that the penance of the indwellers might be the greater. They found shelter with tanned and weather-beaten hermits in their holes and caverns. They poured upon them enthusiastic admiration, and shared with them their Arab bread and clotted milk, and also gave many an alm. Paula fascinated by the desert, would stay there and found a convent. But Jerome prevailed upon her to turn toward Jerusalem.

Thus they came to green Bethlehem, and the calm sweetness of the place and its pleasant fields smote their hearts. Here they determined to settle and build two convents—Jerome's upon the hill near the western gate and Paula's upon the smiling level below. He is said to have sold all that he had, and all that his brother, his faithful and constant companion, had, to gain money for the expense of his building. Paula, doubtless, had ample means from her former great wealth. Indeed, after her own was builded she had two other convents put up near by, and these were soon filled with devotees.

Also, she built a hospice for the reception of travellers, so that, as she said with tender smile and tears in eyes, "If Joseph and Mary should return to Jerusalem, they might be sure of finding room for them in the inn." This gentle speech shines like a gleam of light upon the little holy city, and shows us the noble, natural kindness of Paula, and how profoundly she had been moved by associations to her most sacred and holy. Every poor pilgrim passing her door must to her sympathetic heart have had some semblance to that simple pair who carried the Light of the World to David's little town among the hills.

Paula now laying aside wholly the luxurious habits of her life, set the example of simple and industrious living by washing floors and cleaning lamps and other household work. But she was far from ceasing her studies.

Jerome every day laboured at his great translation, and Paula and Eustochium copied, compared and criticised his daily labours. A great part of the Vulgate he had completed in Rome. His two friends had, doubtless, shared his studies during their long journey. They now read with him every day a portion of the Scriptures in the original; and it was at their entreaty and with their help that he began the translation of the Psalms. The following is a sympathetic description of the method of this work as it was carried out in the rocky chamber at Bethlehem, or in the convent close by:

His two friends charged themselves with the task of collecting all the materials, and this edition, prepared by their care, is that which remains in the Church under Jerome's name.... It is pleasant to think of the two noble Roman ladies seated before the vast desk upon which were spread the numerous manuscripts, Greek, Hebrew and Latin... whilst they examined and compared, reducing to order under their hands, with piety and joy, that Psalter of St. Jerome which is still sung to-day.

So on a whole their days passed in fruitful labour. Jerome held a school for boys and young men, in which he taught the classics. But his great work, and the great work of Paula and Eustochium, was the translation of the Bible into what was then the speech of the people. For this they spared no pains nor costs. They must have found a quiet happiness above all they had calculated in this work. Their minds and thoughts must have been held by the charm of the noble poetry, by the puzzle of words to be cleared and read aright, by the constant interest of accomplishment that every sunrise brought to them, and brings ever to steadfast workers in these days.

And so they dwelt, the gentle Paula, a woman of courtesy, high spirit, steadfastness and gracious, sprightly humour; Eustochium, the grave young daughter who never left her mother's side, whose gentle shadow is one with her mother's; and Jerome, the greatest writer of his time, the mighty controversialist, a man evidently a well of force and sympathy, the kind friend and fellow-worker. Every day the three had conferences as to the most accurate renderings possible, and at all times the greatest respect for the scholarship and acuteness of one another. Amid them was the pleasant stir of independent opinion.

In the books that went forth from that seclusion in Bethlehem we find such an inscription as this:

You, Paula, and Eustochium, who have studied so deeply the books of the Hebrews, take it, this book of Esther, and test it word by word; you can tell whether anything is added, anything withdrawn: and can bear faithful witness whether I have rendered aright in Latin this Hebrew history.

Between these zealous workers in Bethlehem and the old Christian friends in Rome letters were constantly passing. And as the years of her absence grew, Paula, in time, heard of the marriage of Toxotius, who, a little boy of ten, had held out begging hands to her as her ship set sail from the port of Rome. Anon came the joyful news that a daughter had been born and named after her grandmother, Paula. The baby's mother, Leta, looking forward with early longings for the child's future, at once wrote to Jerome about the education of the little one.

The great writer's first thought, amidst his joyous congratulations, is the probable conversion of the baby's maternal grandfather, Albinus, a follower of the old gods.

"Albinus is already a candidate for the faith," he writes, "a crowd of sons and grandsons besiege him. I believe, on my part, that if Jupiter himself had such a family he would be converted to Jesus Christ."

Then Jerome gives, with tender detail, the counsels as to education for which Leta had asked. But he adds:

"It will be difficult to bring up thy little daughter thus at Rome. Send her to Bethlehem; she will repose in the manger of Jesus. Eustochium wishes for her; trust the little one with her. Let this new Paula be cradled on the bosom of her grandmother. Send her to me; I will carry her on my shoulders, old man as I am. I will make myself a child with her; I will lisp to fit her speech; and, believe me, I shall be prouder of my employment than ever Aristotle was of his" [as tutor to Alexander.]

The invitation was accepted. In a few years the little maiden was indeed sent to Bethlehem, though not till after the death of her grandmother Paula. And it was the child, the younger Paula, who at last closed the eyes of Jerome.

Paula, the grandmother, did not live long after the birth of her namesake. Her last illness was beginning. Eustochium watched her night and day, entrusting to no one else the tender last cares—sustaining the drooping head, warming the cold feet, feeding the weakened body, and making the invalid's bed. If the mother fell asleep for a little while, the daughter would go for prayers to the Manger, close at hand and sanctified by its tender associations of motherhood.

But the precious life was slowly ebbing away. Knowing that her end was near, Paula began to repeat with great joy the verses of the Psalms she knew so well:

"Lord, I have loved the habitation of Thy house, and the place where Thine honour dwelleth!"; "How amiable are Thy tabernacles, O Lord God of hosts! My soul longeth, yea, fainteth, for the courts of the house of my God."; "Better to be a doorkeeper in the house of my God than to dwell in the tents of wickedness."

When she had finished, she began to say these songs of the threshold over again. She did not answer when spoken to, until Jerome came and asked gently why she did not speak and if she suffered. Then she answered in Greek, the language of her father and of her childhood, that she had no discomfort, but was "beholding in a vision all quiet and tranquil things." "I feel already an infinite peace," she said. And still she continued to murmur at intervals the words of that ancient song of pilgrimage until her voice grew fainter and fainter, and with the sigh of longing for God's presence on her lips she entered it forever.

All Palestine may be said to have assisted at her funeral. A chorus of psalms and lamentations sounded forth in all languages—Hebrew, Greek, Latin. Hermits crept out of their caves, and monks came in throngs from their monasteries to bewail their generous friend, this great Roman lady, this devoted Christian. During her last days bishops from the neighbouring dioceses had gathered round her and her coffin was borne on their heads into the basilica of the Manger.

And there all the poor, the widowed and orphans lamented "their foster-mother," "their mother," and showed the gifts she had given them and the garments she had made for them. Eustochium could with difficulty be prevailed to leave her. She stayed kissing the cold lips, and at last, her grief breaking through the usual calm of her life, throwing her arms about the unconscious form and praying to be buried beside her.

Paula died at fifty-six. She had spent the last eighteen years of her life in Palestine.

Jerome, for the first time in his laborious life, lost his appetite for work. He could do no more. "I have been able to do nothing, not even from the Scriptures, since the death of the holy and gracious Paula," he wrote. "Grief overwhelms me."

Eustochium, with the instinct of true affection, drew him out of this stupor by inducing him to write a memoir of her mother for her. In two sleepless nights he dictated it. "He could not write himself. Each time that he took up the tablets his fingers stiffened and the stylus fell from his hand. He could not dwell," he said, "on her great pedigree from the Scipios, the Gracchi, from Agamemnon, nor on her splendid opulence and her palace at Rome. She had preferred Bethlehem to Rome. Her praise was that she died poorer than the poorest she had succoured. At Rome she had not been known beyond Rome. At Bethlehem all Christendom, Roman and barbarian, revered her."

"We weep not her loss; we thank God to have had her. Nay! we have her always, for all live by the spirit of God; and the elect who ascend to Him remain still always in the family of those He loves."

Eustochium quietly took up the guidance of her mother's convents and hospice and gently urged Jerome to resume his work. Writing almost countless letters, translating and commenting on the Scriptures he passed still many years, and at last, dying, at his own wish his body was buried in a hollow of the rocks at Bethlehem. To this day, it is said, his name can still be traced graven in the rock.

In the fifteen hundred years that have passed since the death of Paula, the homes of piety and charity established by her strength and love have been swept away. No tradition even of their site is left. But with one storied chamber is connected a warm interest. It is the rocky room, in one of the half caves, half excavations, close to that of the Nativity, and communicating with it by rudely hewn stairs and passages. In this, the legend runs, Jerome established himself while his convent was building. He called it his paradise. Sunlit from above, with prayer and the music of alleluias sounding there night and day, brightened by the glow of the pure affections of Paula and Eustochium and sanctified by their great work, from it flowed rivers of water to refresh the earth.

V

JOAN OF ARC

On the 6th of January, 1412, Jeanne d'Arc, or, as we call her, Joan of Arc, was born at Domremy, a little village on the left bank of the Meuse, on land belonging to the French crown. Her parents, Jacques d'Arc and Isabelle Romée, were simple peasants, "of good life and reputation," who brought up their children to work hard, fear God and honour the saints. Besides Joan, they had four children—three sons, Jacques, Jean and Pierre, and a daughter, Catherine.

Joan's native valley was fair and fertile. The low hills that bounded it were covered with thick forests, and the rich meadows along the Meuse were gay with flowers, which gave to the chief town in the district its name of Vaucouleurs, *Vallis colorum*. Domremy, built on a slope, touched upon those flowery meadows, but over the hill behind it spread an ancient oakwood, the *Bois Chesnu* of legend and prophecy. Between the forest and the village rose solitary a great beech, "beautiful as a lily," about which the country people told a thousand tales. They called it the "Fairies' Tree," the "Tree of the Ladies," the "Beautiful May." In old times the fairies had danced round it, and under its shadow a noble knight had formerly dared to meet and talk with an elfin lady.

But now, in Joan's time, the presence of the fairies was less certain, for the priest of Domremy came once a year to say mass under the tree, and exorcise it and a spring that bubbled up close by. On festival days the young villagers hung it with garlands, danced and played round it, and rested under its boughs to eat certain cakes which their mothers had made for them. During her childhood, Joan brought her cakes and garlands like the rest, danced with them, and sang more than she danced; but as she grew older, she would steal away and carry her flowers to the neighbouring chapel of Our Lady of Domremy.

Her early years were, considering the times, quiet and peaceful. With the war raging between English and French and their allies, to its west and north, Domremy had comparatively little to do. News of English successes, of French defeats, and the sorrows of the French King, were brought by fugitives from the war, by travelling monks, and other wanderers. Joan helped to receive those wayfarers, waited on them, gave up her own bed to them sometimes; and what they told of the woes of France she heard with intense sympathy, and pondered in her heart.

Her bringing up fitted her for the tender fulfilling of all womanly duties. Unlike most girls of her class, she had few outdoor tasks, but spent most of her time at her mother's side, doing the work of the house, learning to sew and spin, to repeat the Belief, and the legends of the saints. Her work done, her dearest pleasure was to go to the village church, which was close to her father's cottage, and there kneel in prayer, gaze on the pictured angels, or listen to the bells calling the faithful to worship: she had always a peculiar delight in the sound of church bells. She fasted regularly, and went often to confession; so often, that her young companions were inclined to jest at her devotion, and even her chosen friends, Haumette and Mengette, half-scolded her for being over-religious. But her faith bore sound fruit. The little money she got she gave in alms. She nursed the sick, she was gentle to the young and weak, obedient to her parents, kind to all. "There was no one like her in the village," said her priest. "She was a good girl," testified an old peasant, "such a daughter as I would gladly have had." A good girl, indeed: they were pure and helpful hands that for a while held the fate of France.

There was a prophecy current during that unhappy time—an old prophecy of Merlin—which the suffering people had taken and applied to their own day and their own need. "The kingdom, lost by a woman, was to be saved by a woman." The woman who had lost it was Isabeau, of Bavaria, the wicked queen, the false wife of Charles VI, the unnatural mother. Who was she that should save it? In the east of France it was said that the deliverer would be a maid from the marshes of Lorraine.

Joan knew the ancient prophecy, and in her young mind it became blended with legends of the saints, with stories of Bible heroines, with her own ardent faith and high aspirations. She loved more and more to be alone. Night and day the wonderful child brooded on the sorrows of France. She sent out her vague hopes and yearnings in tears and prayers, and passionate thoughts that were prayers, and they all came back to her with form and sound, in the visions and voices that were henceforth to be the rulers of her life.

They came first when she was thirteen years old. On a summer's day, at noon, she was in her father's garden, when suddenly by the church there appeared a great light, and out of the light a voice spoke to her, "Joan, be a good child; go often to church." She was frightened then, but both voice and brightness came again and again, and grew dear and familiar. Noble shapes appeared in the glory. St. Michael showed himself to her; St. Catherine and St. Margaret bent over her their radiant heads, bidding her "be good; trust in God." They told her of "the sorrow there was in the kingdom of France," and warned her that one day it would be her mission to go and carry help to the King.

While to outward eyes she lived as usual, she had a life apart, given to God and her saints. She vowed her virginity to Heaven, but of her vow and the visions that had led her to it she told no one, not even the priest. Her meditations, her prayers and unearthly friendships, made of her no sickly dreamer nor hot brained fanatic. She grew up strong, tall and handsome, with a healthy mind in her healthy body.

Meanwhile the dangers of France darkened and thickened. The war was pushing southward; the English leader, Salisbury, was on his way to Orleans; the French King, Charles, poor, indolent, ill-advised, was deliberating whether he should retreat into Dauphiné, or Spain, or Scotland.

Joan's voices grew more frequent and more urgent. Their word now was always, "Go—go into France!" At last they had told her the way: "Go to Vaucouleurs, to Robert de Baudricourt, the governor; he will give you men-at-arms, and send you to the King."

It was now that Joan's trial began. While her beautiful visitors had spoken vaguely of some "deliverance" she was to bring about in the future, she had listened with trembling joy. But now they had plainly shown her the distasteful first step, and for a moment she shrank from taking it. How could a peasant brave the governor of Vaucouleurs? How was a modest girl to venture among rude men-at-arms? How could a dutiful child leave her parents and her home?

"Alas!" she pleaded, "I am a poor girl; I know neither how to ride nor how to fight." She had a short, hard struggle with her own weakness, but the voices did not alter, and she set herself to do their bidding.

Her uncle, Durant Laxart, with whom she evidently was a favourite, lived at a village near Vaucouleurs, and in May, 1428, she went to his house for a visit. After a few days she confided to him something of her plans, reminding him of the old prophecy of Merlin, but never speaking of her visions. With much difficulty she prevailed on him to help her. He went with her to Vaucouleurs, and before the governor, to whom she made known her errand.

"Send and tell the Dauphin," she said, "to wait and not offer battle to his enemies, because God will give him help before mid-Lent. The kingdom belongs not to the Dauphin, but to my Lord; but my Lord wills that the Dauphin shall be king, and hold it in trust. In spite of his enemies he shall be king, and I myself shall lead him to be crowned."

"And who is your Lord?" demanded Baudricourt. She answered, "The King of Heaven."

The governor, a rough and practical soldier, laughed at the young peasant in her coarse red dress, and bade her uncle chastise her well, and take her home to her father.

She returned to Domremy with her heart more than ever fixed on the work she had before her. Now and again she let fall words that revealed enough to make her parents anxious and fearful. Her father dreamed that she had gone away with the soldiers. "If I thought such a thing could happen," he said to her brothers, "I would bid you drown her, and if you refused, I would drown her myself." But she was of a marriageable age; why should she not marry, stay at home, and bring up children, like other women? A lover came forward, a bold one, who, when she rejected him, summoned her before the court at Toul, declaring that she had promised to be his wife. But she went before the judges, spoke out bravely, and defeated her persevering suitor.

As the months passed, her longing increased to be gone and do her voices' bidding. Once more she obtained her uncle's help. His wife was ill, and he came to Domremy and got leave for Joan to go back with him and nurse her. She went, keeping secret the real end of her journey. "If I had had a hundred fathers and a hundred mothers," she said later, "and if I had been a king's daughter, I should have gone." She took leave of her companion Mengette, but to Haumette, her dearer friend, she would not trust herself to say farewell. Her uncle took her to Vaucouleurs, and gave her in charge of a wheelwright's wife, Catherine Royer, with whom she lived for some weeks. She went constantly to church, she helped her hostess in the house, and was gentle and obedient. At the same time, she spoke frankly of her mission to any who chose to hear.

She again went to the governor, who received her no better than before. But she was not cast down.

"I must go to the Dauphin," she said, "though I should go on my knees."

Many people went to see her, among others a brave gentleman of Metz, Jean de Novelonpont.

"What are you doing here, my child?" he asked her, jestingly. "Shall the King be driven out of France, and must we all turn English?"

"I am come to this royal city," she answered, "to bid Robert de Baudricourt take or send me to the King, but he does not heed my words; and yet before mid-Lent I must be before the King, though I should wear away my legs to the knees. For no one else in the world, neither kings, nor dukes, can recover the kingdom of France, and there is no help but in me. And, indeed, I would rather spin with my poor mother, for this is not my calling; but I must go and do it, for it is my Lord's will."

Like Baudricourt, the knight asked her:

"Who is your lord?"

And she answered, "He is God."

But, unlike Baudricourt, he was touched by her words. In the old feudal fashion, he laid his hands within hers and vowed that, by God's help, he would take her to the King. Another worthy gentleman, Bertrand de Poulengy, gave a like promise.

Baudricourt was now forced to listen to Joan. The people of Vaucouleurs believed in her with the ready faith of that time, and she had at least two of his own class to take her part. But those voices of hers, were they of God or of the Devil? Was she witch or saint? The governor, like many another good soldier, had some weakness of superstition. He went to see her, taking with him a priest, who began to exorcise her, bidding her avaunt if she were of the Evil One. Joan approached the priest and knelt before him, honouring not him, but his office; for, as she said afterwards, he had not done well; he should have known that no evil spirit spoke by her.

While she was waiting Baudricourt's pleasure, the Duke of Lorraine, who was ill at Nancy, heard of her, and, hoping for the revelation of some cure, desired to see her. He sent her a safe-conduct, and she went to Nancy under care of her uncle. But she knew only what her voices taught, and she had no power to cure any ills but those of France. This she told the Duke, promising him her prayers, and begging him to aid in her enterprise. He sent her back honourably, but did not pledge himself to the royal cause.

The people of Vaucouleurs came forward to help Joan. They gave her a horse, and the dress and equipment of a soldier; for as she was to travel with men, she wisely chose to wear man's attire. Baudricourt still doubted and delayed. The people she was sojourning with pitied her anxiety. On the day of the battle of Rouvray she went to the governor.

"In God's name," she said, "you are too slow about sending me. To-day the Dauphin has suffered great loss near Orleans, and he is in danger of yet greater if you do not send me to him soon."

At last he yielded to her urgency. He gave her a sword and a letter to the King, and let her prepare to depart. Bertrand de Poulengy, Jean de Novelonpont, and four armed men of lesser rank were to accompany her. She did not see her parents to bid them farewell, but she sent them a letter, entreating them to pardon her. She spoke cheerily to those who were afraid for her safety. God and "her brothers of Paradise" would guard her and her little escort on their dangerous journey.

On February 23, 1429, they set out, Baudricourt bidding her "Go, come of it what may."

Her most timid well-wisher could hardly have exaggerated the perils of the journey. More than half of it was through the enemy's country, where there was continual risk of being stopped and questioned. The rivers, swollen by the winter rains, were unfordable; therefore the travellers had to cross over bridges in full sight of fortified towns.

On the eleventh day of their journey the Maid and her party reached St. Catherine de Fierbois, near Chinon, where they rested, and Joan heard three masses. She sent a letter to Charles requesting an audience, and telling him she had come a hundred and fifty leagues to help him.

An interview with Charles was no such simple affair as she had fancied. Between her and him were doubts, jealousies, intrigues. But her friends prevailed, and after two days' waiting she was admitted to the castle. As she was passing through the gate, a man-at-arms called out,

"What, is that the Maid?" and added a coarse jest and an oath.

Joan turned and looked gravely at him.

"Alas!" she said, "you blaspheme God, and you are so near your death!" Within an hour the man was drowned by accident, and those words of hers were repeated far and wide as a proof of her prophetic power.

The Count of Vendôme led her into the royal presence. She entered meekly, but undismayed; in her visions she had seen finer company than any earthly court could show her. Charles stood among the crowd of nobles, and when she knelt before him he pointed to a richly-dressed lord, saying:

"That is the King, not I."

But she knew the King, probably from descriptions she had heard of him, and answered:

"In God's name, gracious Prince, you are he, and none other." She then repeated to him the words which, like a charm, had brought her so far and overcome so much; "I am Joan the Maid, sent by God to save France," and she asked him for troops, that she might go and raise the siege of Orleans.

Presently the Duke of Alençon came in, and the King having told her who he was, she bade him welcome.

"The more there are of the blood-royal of France," she said, "the better it will be."

Alençon, who had lately returned from a three years' captivity in England, and was still paying a ruinous ransom, sympathised with the girl-champion, and was inclined to believe in her.

The King and his advisers went cautiously to work.

They sent two monks to Domremy to inquire into Joan's character and past life. They called her now and again to Court, where statesmen and churchmen questioned her closely. Meanwhile, she was honourably treated. She was given to the charge of Bellier, the King's lieutenant, whose wife was a lady of virtue and piety, and many distinguished persons visited her at the castle where she was lodged. One day she rode with the lance before the King, and acquitted herself so well that the Duke of Alençon rewarded her with the gift of a beautiful horse. Could she have at all forgotten her mission, the time would have passed pleasantly; as it was, she wearied for action.

At last she sought the King, and said to him:

"Gracious Dauphin"—until Charles was anointed at Reims with the sacred oil, he was no real king in her eyes—"Gracious Dauphin, why will you not believe me? I tell you, God has pity on you, your kingdom and people."

To satisfy all doubts about Joan, it was settled that she should be taken to Poitiers, where the Parliament was assembled, and be there questioned by a royal commission.

"In God's name, let us go," she said; "I shall have hard work, but my Lord will help me."

She was lodged in the house of the advocate-general to the Parliament, and committed to his wife's care. The Archbishop of Reims called together churchmen and learned doctors. The Commissioners met, and, having called Joan, showed her "by good and fair arguments" that she was unworthy of belief. They reasoned with her for more than two hours, and she answered them so well that they were amazed. In spite of their expressed distrust, she spoke to them freely and fully, told how her voices had bidden her go into France, how she had wept at their command and yet obeyed it, how she had come safely, because she was doing the will of God.

"You require an army," said one, "saying it is God's will that the English shall quit France. If that be so, there is no need for men-at-arms, because God can drive them away by His pleasure."

"The men-at-arms shall fight," she answered, "and God shall give the victory"; and the monk confessed that she had answered well.

When the examination had dragged on for three weeks, two of the doctors came one day to question her, bringing with them the King's equerry, whom she had known at Chinon. She clapped him, comrade-like, on the shoulder, exclaiming:

"Would that I had many more men of as good will as you!" Then turning to the doctors, she said, "I believe you are come to catechise me. Listen!—I know neither A nor B, but there is more in God's books than in yours. He has sent me to save Orleans and crown the King."

She demanded paper and ink. "Write what I tell you!" she said, and dictated to the amazed scholars the famous letter which soon after was sent to the English.

The grave and stern commissioners were won by the young peasant. None of them bore her any grudge for the occasional sharpness of her replies. Many of them believed firmly that she was inspired, and quoted the old prophecy of Merlin, who had foretold the coming of a maid who should deliver France. All of them trusted in her good faith, and appreciated more or less the influence she would have over the people. They advised, almost commanded, Charles to employ her. Her life, they said, has been carefully inquired into; for six weeks she has been kept near the King; persons of all ranks, men and women, have seen and talked with her, and have found in her only "goodness, humility, chastity, devotion, seemliness and simplicity." She has promised to show her sign before Orleans: let the King send her there, for to reject her would be to reject the Holy Spirit.

Besides her learned judges, she had others, whom had she been an impostor, she would have found hard to deceive. Keen women's eyes had been set to watch her, and had seen no fault in her. The ladies who came to see the warrior-damsel were amazed to find her a mere girl, "very simple, and speaking little." Her goodness and innocence moved them to tears. She prayed them to pardon her for the man's attire she wore; but in that lawless day the most modest women must have well understood that such a dress was fittest and safest for her who had to live among men.

Towards the end of April she was sent to Tours, where a military staff was appointed her. Her brothers, Jean and Pierre, who had followed her, were included in her retinue. A suit of beautiful armour was made for her. She was provided with a banner after her own device—white, embroidered with lilies: on one side of it, a picture of God enthroned on clouds and holding a globe in His hand; on the other, the shield of France, supported by two angels. She had also a pennon, whereon was represented the Annunciation. The King would have given her a sword, but her voices, she said, had told her of the only one she might use, an ancient weapon with five crosses on its blade, which was lying buried behind the altar in the church of St. Catherine de Fierbois. A messenger was sent, and in the place she had told of was found an old rusty sword such as she had described. After being polished, it was brought to her with two rich scabbards, one of crimson velvet, the other of cloth-of-gold; but the practical Maid got herself yet another of strong leather for daily wear.

Joan, being accepted, the National party made rapid preparations for the relief of Orleans.

Her first care was that the army given her by God should be worthy of His favour. For the priests attached to it, she had a banner made with a picture of the Crucifixion, beneath which they said mass and sang hymns to the Virgin morning and evening.

On Thursday, April 28th, the relieving army set out from Blois, the priests going before and singing the *Veni Creator* round their banner of the Cross. Joan wished to march along the north bank of the Loire, and through the line of English forts; her voices, she said, had told her that the convoy would pass them without hurt. But the captains, who had little faith in her revelations, preferred keeping the river between themselves and the chief bastiles of the enemy. They had orders, however, to obey the Maid, so, to avoid contradicting her, they misled her as to the position of Orleans; crossing the bridge at Blois, they advanced by the south bank of the stream. When night came, the army encamped on the plain, and Joan, who lay down in her armour, arose bruised and weary for the next day's march. But all her fatigue was forgotten when she saw how she had been deceived.

Dunois, with a following of knights and citizens, came up the river to welcome the convoy. When he approached Joan, she asked him:

"Are you the bastard of Orleans?"

"Yes," he replied, "and I am glad of your coming."

"And did you advise that I should be brought by this side of the river, and not straight to the English?"

He answered that it was so, he and the council having judged it safest.

"In God's name," she said, "my Lord's counsel is safer and wiser than yours. You thought to deceive me, but you have deceived yourselves, for I bring you the best help that ever knight or city had; for it is God's help, not sent for love of me, but by God's pleasure."

At eight that evening she entered Orleans, riding a white horse, her standard carried before her. The people thronged to meet her, wild with joy, "as if she had been an angel of God." "They felt comforted and, as it were, dis-besieged by the divine virtue there was said to be in that simple Maid." They crowded so upon her, that one of their torches set fire to the border of her standard, and when she bent forward and crushed out the flame, the little brave action seemed a miracle to the excited multitude. After returning thanks to God in the cathedral, she rode to the house of Jacques Boucher, treasurer to the Duke of Orleans, and was hospitably received by his wife and his young daughter Charlotte, whom she took to share her chamber during her stay in the city.

The next Sunday, May 1st, Dunois went to fetch the army from Blois. The Maid rode with him a little way, and he and his following passed unmolested by the English forts. The days of his absence were spent by Joan in making friends with the citizens, in attending mass and riding out to reconnoitre the enemy's siege-works. The enthusiastic people followed her everywhere, fearing nothing so long as they were near her. On Tuesday some reinforcements arrived, and news came that the army was on its way.

This time they took the northern side of the river, and on May 4th Joan went a league out of the city to meet them. The whole army passed the line of forts and entered Orleans. The besiegers made no sign, and it is not wonderful that the English soldiers, seeing that strange apathy of their leaders, believed Joan to be a witch, whose arts it would be useless to resist.

The same day, towards evening she lay down to rest, but suddenly she started up and called her squire, saying, "My counsel tells me to go against the English." While he was arming her, she heard voices in the street shouting that the French were suffering loss. She rushed out, and meeting her page on the way:

"Ah, graceless boy!" she exclaimed, "you never told me the blood of France was being spilt."

Her hostess finished arming her, then she sprang upon her horse, took her standard which the page handed her out of a window, and galloped to the eastern gate, her horse's hoofs striking sparks as she passed.

For the first time she now saw real war, and her courage did not fail. Standing at the edge of the fosse, she urged her men on to the assault. This first success, moderate in itself, was of immense value to the National party, for it restored to the French that faith in themselves of which the long series of their defeats had almost deprived them. And their reverse had as great an effect upon the English. Their failure appeared to them out of the natural course of events, a wicked miracle, a thing brought about by sorcery. The brave yeomen of Henry V were learning to fear.

On Friday, May 6th, Joan and about 3,000 men crossed to an island, in the Loire, passed from it to the shore by an extempore bridge of two boats, and planted her standard before the rampart of the Augustins. But her troops had not all crossed from Orleans, and those who were with her, seeing that the English were coming to reinforce their fellows, were seized with fear, and hurried back to the boats. The garrison rushed out and pursued the fugitives with jeers and insults. The defeat of the French appeared certain, but Joan, who had been trying to cover the retreat, faced round, and with a small brave company charged the pursuers. The panic was on their side now. They saw the Witch of France riding down upon them, her charmed standard flying, her eyes flashing with terrible wrath, and they turned and fled before her. Once more she planted her flag before the rampart, and this time she was well supported. The bastile was taken after an obstinate defence, and to prevent riot and pillage she ordered it to be set on fire.

She would gladly have stayed with her soldiers who were left that night to be ready for the next day's assault, but the chiefs, seeing that she was very weary, persuaded her to return with them into Orleans. They had another reason for parting her from the troops. While she was resting they held a council, and agreed not to renew the attack on the morrow, but recall the troops into the city, which was now well victualled, and there await reinforcements. A knight was sent to tell her of their over-cautious decision:

"God had already done much to help them; now they would wait." Wait!—how Joan must have hated that word! "You have been in your council," she said, "and I have been in mine. Be sure that God's counsel will hold good and come to pass, and that all other counsel shall perish."

Then she turned to Pasquerel, who was standing near.

"Rise early to-morrow," she said, "and keep near me all day, for I shall have much to do, and blood shall flow above my breast."

She rose at dawn, and after hearing mass, started for the assault. Her host urged her to take food before going; a shad was being got ready, he told her.

"Keep it till evening," she said, gaily, "I will come back over the bridge."

If the French fought for the deliverance of Orleans and the kingdom, the English were defending their ancient glory and their own lives; the fort once taken, there would be small chance of escape for any of its garrison. Under cannon-fire and through flights of arrows, the assailants leaped into the fosse and swarmed up the escarpment, "as if they believed themselves immortal."

The English met them at the top; again and again they were driven back, again and again the Maid cheered them on, crying:

"Fear not!—the place is yours!"

At last, as if to force victory, she sprang into the fosse, and was setting a scaling-ladder against the wall when an arrow pierced her between the neck and shoulder. She was carried to a place of shelter, weeping for pain and fright; but her strong courage soon reasserted itself; she drew out the arrow with her own hand, and had the wound dressed with oil, forbidding the men-at-arms to "charm" it, as they in their superstitious kindness wanted to do. She then confessed herself, and so, hastened back to the rampart.

There was no success yet for the French, and the captains came to Joan, telling her they intended to retire and suspend the attack until next day. She besought them to persevere. She tried to break their resolve with brave words. She went to Dunois with prayers and promises.

"In God's name, you shall enter shortly. Doubt not, and the English shall have no more power over you!"

Her entreaties prevailed. Then she ordered the men to rest a while, eat and drink, and when they had done so, bade them renew the attack "in God's name."

She mounted her horse again and rode to a vineyard a little way off, where, out of the turmoil of battle, she prayed a few minutes. On her return she stationed herself near the rampart, holding her standard.

"Watch until my banner touches the fort," she said to a gentleman who stood near. Presently the wind caught it and blew it against the wall.

"It touches, Joan, it touches!" exclaimed the gentleman.

She cried to the troops:

"Go in now, all is yours!"

By evening Joan reëntered Orleans, where she and her men were received with great joy, all the bells of the city ringing out the news of victory. The Maid's wound was dressed carefully, and after her usual supper of bread with a little wine and water, she lay down to sleep.

Very early next morning, those watching in Orleans saw the English quit their bastiles and set themselves before the walls in order of battle. The alarm was given, and the French, led by Joan, came out of the city and ranged themselves in front of their enemies. While the armies stood face to face, as it were waiting for a signal to begin to fight, Joan had a camp-altar brought, and the priests said mass. Then she asked:

"Are the faces of the English towards us, or their backs?"

She was told that they were retreating, and at that moment flames shot up from some of their forts which they had set on fire.

"In God's name," said Joan, "let them go. My Lord does not choose that we shall fight to-day. You shall have them another time."

Crowds rushed out from Orleans to destroy the unburnt bastiles, and dragged back the stores and cannon the English had been obliged to leave. But soon the excitement of victory gave way to the enthusiasm of thankfulness. A few days ago the city had been surrounded by enemies, threatened with the sword, more than threatened by famine. But in one marvellous week God and the Maid had delivered it. Now let her who had led the people to victory lead them also to give thanks. They thronged after her. They followed her from church to church, praising God and the saints, God and the Maid, before their rescued altars. Night fell on their rejoicings, and early next morning the Maid left them, eager to rejoin the King, and render an account of her success. Her time for rest was not yet. She had as yet only given the sign promised to the doctors of Poitiers—only begun the great work she was sent to do.

Scholars, high in place, great in learning, paid her their tribute of praise. But the common people were her most eager admirers and lovers. During her journey from Orleans to Tours, they crowded about her, trying to touch her hands, her dress, the trappings of her horse—even stooping down to kiss the hoof-prints of her horse on the road.

Charles came to meet her at Tours. When she knelt before him, he took off his cap, as to a queen, raised her, and seemed "as if he gladly would have kissed her, for the joy he had." He would have ennobled her at once, and he desired her to take for her arms the lilies of France, with a royal crown and a sword drawn to defend it. Empty honours and easy lip-gratitude were at her service, but she, who had only one noble ambition, cared nothing for them. She wanted but one boon from the King—ready action. Now was the time to go to Reims, while the English were weakened and disheartened. Let the King come—she would conduct him there safely and without hindrance—but let him come at once, for she had much to do, and little time wherein to do it.

"Make use of me," she pleaded, "for I shall last only one year."

Her bold proposal amazed Charles and his council. Go to Reims, to a city held by the English, through a country guarded by hostile troops!

The King, half-persuaded, agreed to go, but not until the English had been driven from the Loire. The captains declared that it would be unwise to march northward while the southern provinces remained so exposed to the enemy, and Joan, whose good sense equalled her courage, deferred to their judgment. An army was assembled, and put under command of the Duke of Alençon, but the King required him to do nothing without the Maid's advice. While she was near Charles, and her brave words were in his ears, he almost believed in her.

On the 9th of June, just a month after her departure from Orleans, Joan returned there with her army. During the campaign she made the city her headquarters, to the delight of its people, who "could not have enough of gazing at her." On the 11th she led the troops against Jargeau, a strong town, bravely defended, but the assailants had the advantage of numbers, and, once their fears were forgotten, went boldly to the attack. Joan and the Duke, commanders though they were, went down into the fosse like the rest, and the Maid was climbing a scaling-ladder, when a stone hurled from the rampart struck her to the earth. But she was up in a moment, shouting:

"Friends, friends, go on! Our Lord has condemned the English! They are ours! Be of good courage!" The men swarmed over the walls, and the place was taken. The more important captives were sent down the Loire to Orleans, where Joan and Alençon returned the day after their victory. Soon after, near Patay they came upon the English, who had been warned of their approach, and were getting ready for battle. The Duke asked Joan what was to be done.

"Have you good spurs?" she inquired.

"What!" exclaimed some who stood by; "should we turn our backs?"

"Not so, in God's name!" she answered. "The English shall do that. They will be beaten, and you will want your spurs to pursue them."

Some of the chiefs hung back.

"In God's name, we must fight them!" she cried. "Though they were hung to the clouds, we should have them. To-day the King shall have the greatest victory he has won for long. My counsel tells me they are ours."

In slain and prisoners the English lost nearly 3,000 men. Joan was very indignant at the cruelty of the victors. Seeing one of them strike down a wounded prisoner she sprang from her horse, raised the poor soldier in her arms, and held him thus while he confessed to a priest whom she had sent for, tenderly comforting him until he died. It was always so with her. Before and during the fight she was the stern champion of France; but when it was over she became again a pitying woman, weeping for her dead enemies, and praying for their souls.

Now Joan held her rightful place in the army. Every true and honest man believed in her; even those who had doubted her at Orleans confessed now not only her goodness and courage, but also the instinctive military skill she had shown both in sieges and in the field. Soldiers and leaders were alike eager to follow her to Reims. With nothing to consult and combat but their frank likes and dislikes, her task would have been an easy one; but to do her voices' bidding, she had to hew or wind her way through the intrigues of a court.

Charles demurred at going to Reims at all. He hated trouble, and his life in the south had been pleasant enough. All Joan's victories had as yet done him no substantial good. He was as poor as ever, and the excited men who flocked to the Maid's banner were to him objects less of pride than of distrust.

The Maid, foreseeing more delays, sick at heart of his apathy, could not control her tears, and he, bewildered by a grief he could not understand, spoke to her kindly, paid her many compliments, and advised her to take some rest. Still weeping, she besought him to have faith, promising that he should recover his kingdom and be crowned before long.

On Friday, June 24th, she brought the army of the Loire to Gien, whence she sent a letter to the loyal city of Tournay, telling its people of her late successes, and praying them to come to the coronation.

Two days after her arrival at Gien, the justly impatient girl quitted the town with some of her troops and encamped in the fields beyond it. Her persistence carried the day. On the 29th, the King and an army of 12,000 men set out for Reims.

On July 5th it reached Troyes. Joan had written to the citizens, requiring them to receive the King, and Charles also bade them surrender, promising them amnesty and easy terms. But the place was well garrisoned, and they determined to resist.

A council was held, and nearly all who were at it advised returning southward. But among those faint hearts was one man who believed in Joan—the old chancellor—and he spoke boldly for her. "When the King undertook this journey, he did it not because of the great might of the men-at-arms, nor because of the great wealth he had, nor because the journey seemed possible to him, but because Joan told him to go forward and be crowned at Reims, such being the good pleasure of God." While he was yet speaking, Joan herself knocked at the door. She was let in, and the Archbishop told her the cause of the debate.

She turned to the King.

"Will you believe me?" she asked.

"Speak," he replied, "and if you speak reasonably and profitably, we will gladly believe you."

"Will you believe me?" she said again.

"Yes," repeated Charles, "according to what you say."

That cold answer might well have checked her, but she spoke on:

"Gracious King of France, if you will remain before your city of Troyes, it shall be yours within three days by force or by love—doubt it not."

"We would wait six, if we could be sure of having it," said the Archbishop.

"Doubt not," she insisted, "you shall have it to-morrow."

It was then evening, but she at once mounted her horse and began preparations for an assault. Her energy cheered the soldiers, who were weary of inaction. They dragged the cannons into position, and brought bundles of wood, doors, furniture, everything they could lay hands on, to fill up the fosse. They worked far into the night—leaders, pages, men-at-arms alike—Joan directing them "better than two of the best captains could have done."

Through that night there was great excitement within Troyes. The people had heard of Orleans and Jargeau; they could see and hear Joan's preparations. At last they asked loudly why they, French by birth, should risk their city and their lives for England. A council was held, and the heads of the garrison and the city agreed to surrender. Early next morning, just as Joan was giving the signal for the assault, the city gates were opened.

The next day, Sunday, the King entered the town in state, attended by Joan and his nobles.

They left Troyes, and approached Châlons on the 15th, and at some distance from the town were met by a number of citizens who had come to offer their submission. At Châlons, Joan had the great joy of meeting friends from Domremy. She asked them many questions about her home, and they looked with wonder at the girl who lived familiarly with princes, and yet spoke and behaved as simply as ever she had done in the days of her obscurity. One of them inquired whether she feared nothing.

"Nothing but treachery," was her foreboding answer.

When the people of Reims heard that Châlons had submitted, and that Charles was within four leagues, they sent deputies to tender their obedience, and that same day, Saturday, July 16th, Charles entered the city.

Preparations were at once made for his coronation, and early next morning four nobles went to the abbey of St. Rémi to escort thence the ampulla containing the sacred oil which a dove had brought from heaven to the saint. The abbot, in full canonicals, carried it to the cathedral, where the Archbishop of Reims received it from him, and set it on the high altar. Below the altar stood the Dauphin, attended by the nobles and clergy who acted as proxies for the peers of France who should have been with him. By his side was Joan, holding her sacred banner. The ceremony was performed according to the ancient rites, and when it was over, Joan knelt at the feet of Charles, her King indeed now, crowned and anointed.

"Gracious King," she said, "now is fulfilled the pleasure of God, whose will it was that you should come to Reims to receive your worthy coronation, showing that you are the true King to whom the kingdom should belong." As she spoke she wept, and all who were in the church wept for sympathy. Among those who witnessed her triumph was her father, who had come to Reims to see her. The good man was honourably treated; the corporation of the town paid his expenses, and when he returned to Domremy, gave him a horse for the journey.

After his coronation, when Charles was bestowing honours and rewards on his followers, Joan asked him for one favour, which he granted readily—freedom from taxation for her native Domremy and the adjoining village of Greux. For herself she wanted nothing, except what she had already claimed and failed to receive, what the King never gave her—his trust.

She had given a king to France, now she had to give France to her King. She longed to be again at work. Every day of waiting was a day of pain to her. Now that her King was crowned, she would have him press forward to Paris, defy the English, and startle the disloyal French into loyalty; but the evil advice of his courtiers and his own indolence made him catch at every excuse for delay.

During the northward march of the army, people from every place on the road crowded to welcome Joan and the King, crying, Noël, Noël, and singing *Te Deums* before them. Joan was first. They were glad to have a French King again, but their chief love and enthusiasm were for her, the heroic girl in shining armour, with her calm face and gentle voice. The common folk called her "the angelic"; they sang songs about her; images of her were put up in little country churches; a special collect was said at mass, thanking God for her having saved France; medals were struck in her honour, and worn as amulets. The people pressed about her horse, and kissed her hands and feet. She was often vexed by this excess of homage, which brought upon her the displeasure of many churchmen.

Near Crespy, as she, riding between Dunois and Regnault de Chartres, passed through the welcoming crowd, she said:

"What good people! I have yet seen none so joyful at the coming of their prince. May I be so happy as to die and be buried in this land!"

"Oh, Joan," said the Archbishop, "in what place do you expect to die?"

"Wherever it shall please God," she answered, "for I know not the place nor the hour any more than yourself. Would to God that I might return now, and lay down my arms, and go back to serve my parents, and guard their flocks with my sister and brothers, who would be right glad to see me." She must often have longed for her home, but never except this once did she express her longing. She had a rare reticence for one so young and simple. "She spoke little, and showed a marvellous prudence in her words."

Joan greatly desired the King's arrival before Paris, believing that his mere presence would make its gates fly open like those of Reims and Soissons. The King's folly and the ill-will of his favourites were not Joan's only troubles. The army before Paris was not like that chosen army she had led to Orleans, a company of men "confessed, penitent," who for the time seemed purified from evil desires, and followed her as to a holy war. Such a state of things, fair to the eye, but born only of the froth and ecstasy of religion, could not last, as the Maid in her young confidence perhaps expected. She had now to grieve because of her soldiers' habits of blasphemy and pillage.

On the morning of September 8th, the festival of the Virgin's nativity, they advanced to attack the city. They were divided into two corps. One, led by Joan, Gaucourt, and Retz, went at once to the assault. The attack began about noon; the bastion of the St. Honoré gate having been set on fire, its defenders were forced to abandon it, and the assailants, headed by Joan, passed the outer fosse. She climbed the ridge separating it from the inner fosse, which was full of water, and from that place summoned the city to surrender. She was answered with jeers and insults and a shower of missiles, amid which she carefully sounded the fosse with her lance, and found that it was of unusual depth. At her bidding the men brought faggots and hurdles to fill it up and make a resting-place for their ladders, but while she was directing them, an arrow wounded her in the thigh so severely that she was forced to lie down at the edge of the fosse. She suffered, as she afterwards confessed, agonies of pain, but she never ceased to encourage her men, bidding them advance boldly, for the place would be taken. The place would have been taken, but the captains who were with Joan, seeing that the hours went by and the men were struck down without achieving much, ordered a retreat. The trumpets sounded; the men withdrew, Joan, desperate in her sorrow, clung to the ground, declaring she would not go until the place was won. At about ten o'clock Gaucourt had her removed by force and set upon her horse. She was carried back to La Chapelle, suffering in body, suffering more in mind, but still resolute.

"The city would have been taken!" she insisted. "It would have been taken!"

Joan spent four weary months—how weary we conjecture chiefly from what we know of her character and her aspirations.

Occasionally she rode with a few followers to visit some town where she was known, but generally she was with the Court, a sad and unwilling spectator of its festivities. Sad only because of her unfulfilled mission: had she been suffered to work it out, to see France delivered, she would doubtless have taken pleasure in show and gaiety. She was at home and happy with knights and ladies, and took a frank delight in rich garments and fine armour. She was no bigot, her sanctity was altogether wholesome: it was an exalted love for God, for France and the King, unsoured by any contempt for the common life of humanity.

Wherever she went she visited the sick, she gave all she could in alms, she was devoted to the services of the church and to prayer. The people, who knew of her greatness and saw her goodness, treated her with a reverence that was akin to superstition. They brought rings and crosses for her to touch, and so turn into amulets. "Touch them yourselves," she would say, laughing, "they will be just as good." Some believed that she had a charmed life, and need never fear going into battle.

Joan grew desperate. Sad voices from beyond the Loire were calling her. She was greatly wanted there, and the King—her King whom she had crowned—did not want her, cared nothing for her nor for his people's trouble. She asked counsel of her other voices, of her saints, and they neither bade her go nor stay; they told her only one certain thing, that before St. John's day she would be taken. If so—if indeed, as she herself had said, she was to last only a year—then the more need to hasten with her work. One day at the end of March she left Sully with a small company, as if going for one of her usual rides. She did not bid farewell to the King, and she never saw him again.

It was a time of sad forebodings for her. A story goes, that one morning, after hearing mass in the church of St. Jacques, she went apart and leaned dejectedly against a pillar. Some grown people and a crowd of children came about her—she was always gentle to children—and she said to them:

"My children and dear friends, I tell you that I am sold and betrayed, and that I shall soon be given up to death. Therefore I entreat you to pray for me, for never again shall I have any power to serve the King or the Kingdom of France." She was not "sold and betrayed" yet; that was to come.

Depression could not make her inactive. She went to Crespy for reinforcements, but hearing that the siege of Compiègne had begun, she hurried back there on the night of April 23rd, with about four hundred men. She entered the place at sunrise, and spent the chief part of the day in arranging a sortie, to be made before evening. Compiègne, situated on the south bank of the Oise, was connected with the opposite shore by a bridge, from which a raised causeway went over the low river meadows to the hill-slopes of Picardy.

Late in the afternoon, Joan, with five hundred foot and horsemen, made a short charge. Then Joan's troops feared to be cut off from Compiègne, to be left in a country dotted with the enemy's camps, and most of them turned, panic-stricken, and fled towards the city.

The English gained the causeway, and the archers stationed there dared not shoot on them for fear of hurting their own people. The guns of Compiègne were useless, for friends and foes were mingled in a confused struggle. Joan tried to rally her men:

"Hold your peace!" she cried to some who spoke of retreating. "It depends on you to discomfit them! Think only of falling upon them!"

But her words were in vain. All she could do was to cover the retreat, and that she did valiantly, riding last, and charging back often. Thanks to her a great part of the fugitives got safely into the city, while others reached the boats; but the English pressed towards the gate to cut off the retreat of the remainder, and Guillaume de Flavy, afraid, as he said, lest in the confusion they might rush into the town itself, ordered the draw-bridge to be raised, and the portcullis lowered. There was no escape for the Maid now. She and a little devoted band that kept with her fought desperately, but they were driven into an angle of the fortifications; many fell in defending her.

Compiègne remained shut. The city to whose help she had come at dawn saw her lost at its very gates before sundown, and made no effort to save her. Five or six men rushed on her at once, each crying:

"Yield to me! Pledge your faith to me!"

"I have sworn and pledged my faith to another than you," she said, "and I will keep my oath."

She still struck at those who tried to seize her; but an archer came behind her, and, grasping the gold-embroidered surcoat that she wore, dragged her from her horse. She fell, exhausted and overcome at last, and the man who had pulled her down carried her to his master.

She was taken to Margny, and thither flocked the English and Burgundian captains, "more joyful than if they had taken five hundred fighting men." In this very month of her capture, it had been found needful to issue proclamations against English soldiers, men of the old conquering race, who had refused to come over to France for fear of the Witch. And now here was the Witch, vanquished, powerless, her armour soiled in the fight, her magic banner fallen away from her. The chiefs could hardly believe their good fortune, but her sad presence was there to assure them of it, and they came and gazed on her.

The weeks went by, and no one stirred to help her. Her captors' scruples were overcome, and before winter she was bought and sold. John of Luxembourg got ten thousand livres— two thousand dollars.

*　　*　　*　　*　　*

Hitherto we have seen Joan, a gracious figure always—better always and nobler than her surroundings—but never yet solitary in goodness and nobleness. Other figures have been grouped about her, gracious also in their degree, worthy to divide with her our sympathy, and to have some share in our love. Now they are all gone from her. Father and mother, village friends and kinsfolk, devoted comrades and adoring people, are all shut away from her for ever. The old life is over.

She is desolate, and worse than alone; to the darling of the saints, loneliness would be no such terrible punishment. Wrong and horror crowd upon her. Her honour and her life are in the hands of men evil by nature, or turned to evil by hatred, or greed, or fear. Here and there a judge speaks some word in favour of banished justice, but those feeble flashes leave no light in the gloom. The light shines all on Joan. The pure maiden, the noble heroine, stands out, heaven-illumined, against the darkness. Her sorrow and her endurance of it crown and sanctify her. Piteous though her fate be, we almost forget to pity her, for compassion is well-nigh lost in reverence and wonder.

On her arrival at Rouen, Joan was taken to the castle, and put into an iron cage that had been made to receive her; and, as if its bars were not enough, she was chained in it by her neck, her hands and her feet. After being kept thus for several days, she was transferred to a gloomy chamber in one of the towers, where she was fettered to a great log of wood during the day, and to her bed at night. Both by night and day she was guarded by five English soldiers of the lowest and rudest class, three of whom were always with her, while the other two kept the door outside.

Once given over to the Church, she should have been placed in an ecclesiastical prison, and guarded by women. For this right she pleaded often, and her plea was supported by several of her judges. But the English would not lose their grip of a captive who had cost them and lost them so much, and Pierre Cauchon, Bishop of Beauvais, had too great fear of displeasing them to advise such a simple measure of decency and justice.

Joan had visitors in her prison. English nobles whose nobility did not keep them from insulting a woman and a helpless captive, came to stare and jest at her. Warwick and Stafford came one day, and with them a man who might well have shrunk from looking her in the face—the Judas of Luxembourg. He told her he had come to ransom her, on condition that she would not again take up arms against England. She answered him scornfully, as he deserved:

"In God's name, you but mock me, for I know you have neither the will nor the power to do it;" and she added, "I know that the English will kill me, thinking to have the kingdom of France after my death; but were they a hundred thousand Goddams more than they are, they should not have the kingdom."

Cauchon refused the Maid's just request for counsel to advise and defend her during her examination. But he was not merciful enough to leave her to the guidance of her own wise brain and true heart. According to the bad custom of the Inquisition, he sent her a sham confidant, a creature even more abject than himself—his friend and tool, the Canon Loyseleur. This man went to Joan in disguise, and told her that he, too, was a prisoner, a loyal subject of King Charles, and a native of her own province. The guards left them together, and she, poor child! being glad to see a friendly face, talked to him with a trustfulness that might have touched even such a heart as his. The bishop listened in an adjoining room, and stationed two scribes there to report Joan's words; but the men were too honest for such work, and refused to do it. To gain her fuller confidence, Loyseleur made known to her that he was a priest, and heard her in confession. He also gave her counsel how to answer her judges— bad and crooked counsel, of which she availed herself little, but still enough for us to trace here and there the influence of an evil mind over hers.

On Tuesday, February 20th, she was summoned to appear next day before her judges. Having heard and seen what they were, she demanded that an equal number of assessors of the French party should be associated with them. She also entreated the Bishop of Beauvais to let her hear religious service. The prayer was denied.

Joan appeared before them a youthful, girlish creature in her masculine dress. The dress was all black, relieved only by the pale prison-worn face, from which the dark eyes looked out fearlessly.

The bishop began by briefly stating the crimes she was accused of, and explaining to her how he came to be her judge. He then exhorted her, "with gentleness and charity," to answer truly all questions put to her. From the first moment of the trial she was on her guard. She felt her judges' falsehood and malevolence in the very air around her.

The Gospels were brought, and she was ordered to swear upon them that she would speak the truth. She hesitated.

"I do not know what questions you may put to me," she said. "Perhaps you will ask me things I cannot tell you."

"Will you swear," insisted Cauchon, "to speak the truth about whatever you are asked concerning the faith, and whatever you know?" She answered that she would willingly speak of her parents, and of all her own actions since she had left Domremy.

Jean Beaupère took up the examination. His first question was, when she had last eaten and drunk. It was the season of Lent; if she had taken food as usual, she might be accused of contempt for the Church; if she had fasted, she gave colour to a theory of Beaupère's, that her visions were induced chiefly by physical causes. She told him she had fasted since noon the day before. He inquired at what hour she had last heard the voice.

"I heard it yesterday and to-day," she said. "I was asleep, and it woke me.... I do not know whether it was in my room, but it was in the castle.... I thanked it, sitting up in my bed, with clasped hands, and implored its counsel.... I had asked God to teach me by its counsel how to answer."

"And what did the voice say?"

"It told me to answer boldly, and God would help me." Here she turned to the bishop. "You say that you are my judge. Take heed what you do, for indeed I am sent by God, and you are putting yourself in great peril."

Beaupère asked her if the voice never varied in its counsel.

"No," she said; "it has never contradicted itself. Last night again it bade me answer boldly."

Her dress, her banner and pennon, were inquired about. Had not the Knights, her companions, their pennons made after the pattern of hers? Had she not told them that such pennons would be lucky? To this she answered:

"I said to my men—'Go in boldly among the English!'—*and I went myself.*"

"Did you not tell them to carry their pennons boldly, and they would have good luck?"

"I indeed told them what came to pass, and will come to pass again."

Had she not ordered pictures or images of herself to be made? No, nor had she ever seen any image in her likeness. She had seen a picture of herself at Arras. She was represented kneeling on one knee, and presenting letters to the King.

Did she know that those of her party had caused masses and prayers to be said in her honour?

"I know nothing of it," she answered, "and if they did so, it was not by my command. Nevertheless, if they prayed for me, I think they did no wrong."

"Do those of your party believe firmly that you are sent by God?"

"I do not know. I leave that to their consciences. But if they do not believe it, I am none the less sent by Him."

"Do you think them right in believing it?"

"If they believe that I am sent by God, they are not deceived."

"Did you understand the feelings of those who kissed your feet, your hands and your garments?"

"Many were glad to see me. I let them kiss my hands as little as possible; but the poor people came to me gladly, because I did them no unkindness, but helped them as much as I could."

"Did not the women touch their rings with the ring you wore?"

"Many women touched my hands and my rings, but I do not know why they did so."

* * * * *

For more than three months her trial went on. But her fate was settled now. The Inquisition had no pardon for her. The judges left her, a few daring to be sorry for the brave creature, but most of them openly and indecently glad. In the courtyard they found a number of English waiting for news, among them the Earl of Warwick.

"Farewell, farewell!" cried the bishop, as he passed him; "be of good cheer—it is done!"

Her guilt was proved; let her be given over to the secular power; but first let her be charitably exhorted for her soul's welfare, and warned that she had nothing more to hope for in this world.

The bishop ordered a citation to be drawn up, summoning Joan to appear next morning in the Old Market Place of Rouen, to receive her final sentence. She did not hear her doom that night (May 30, 1431), but the grave faces and grave words of the monks showed her the dreadful reality, and for a little while youth and womanhood and human weakness had their own way with her. She wept piteously.

"Alas," she cried, "will they treat me so horribly and cruelly? Must my body be consumed to-day and turned to ashes? Ah! I would sooner seven times be beheaded than be burnt! Oh, I appeal to God, the great Judge, against the wrong and injustice done to me!"

While she was thus lamenting Cauchon came in, with Pierre Maurice, and two or three others. Seeing him, she cried:

"Bishop, I die by you!"

Maurice looked kindly at her as he went, and she said to him:

"Master Pierre, where shall I be to-night?"

"Have you not a good hope in God?" he asked.

"Ah, yes, and by God's grace, I shall be in Paradise."

She received the sacrament with tears, and with deep penitence and devotion. Thenceforth her faith was unshaken, and she failed no more.

Next morning at nine o'clock she left the prison, clothed now in a woman's long gown, and wearing a mitre, inscribed with the words, *Heretic, Relapsed, Apostate, Idolatress.* A cart was waiting for her, and she got into it, accompanied by Brother Martin and the usher Massieu. A guard of about eight hundred soldiers surrounded her to keep off the crowd, but suddenly there rushed through their ranks a haggard and miserable figure. It was Nicolaus Loyseleur, who, seized by late and vain remorse, had come to ask forgiveness of her whom he had betrayed. But before he could reach her, the soldiers drove him back, and Joan probably neither saw nor heard him, for she was weeping and praying, her head bowed upon her hands.

When she looked up, she saw beyond the soldiers a dense throng of people, most of them grieving for her, many of them lamenting that this thing should be done in their city.

"O Rouen, Rouen!" she cried, "is it here that I must die?"

At last she reached the Old Market Place, a very large space, where had been raised three scaffolds: one for the Bishop of Beauvais and his colleagues, and for all the prelates and nobles who desired to see the show; another for Joan and some priests and officials; the third, also for Joan—a pile of stone and plaster, raised high above the heads of the crowd, and heaped with faggots. In front of it was a tablet bearing this inscription:

Joan, who has called herself The Maid—liar, pernicious, deceiver of the people, sorceress, superstitious, blasphemer of God, presumptuous, disbeliever of the faith of Christ, boaster, idolatress, dissolute, invoker of devils, apostate, schismatic, heretic.

Master Nicolas Midi, a famous doctor from Paris, preached Joan's last sermon, on the text, "If one member suffer, all the members suffer with it."

At its close, he addressed her:

"Joan, go in peace! The Church can no longer defend you; it gives you up to the secular power."

Then the bishop spoke to her. He did not read the form of abjuration, as had been advised, for she would have boldly disavowed it, and would so have spoilt a scheme he had concocted. But he admonished her to think of her salvation, to remember her misdeeds, and repent of them. Finally, after the usual inquisitorial form, he declared her cut off from the Church, and delivered over to secular justice.

She needed no exhortation to prayer and penitence. For a while she seemed to forget the gazing crowd and the cruel judges. She knelt and prayed fervently—prayed aloud with such passionate pathos, that all who heard her were moved to tears. Even Cauchon wept. Even the Cardinal was touched. She forgave her enemies; she remembered the King, who had forgotten her; she asked pardon of all, imploring all to pray for her, and especially entreating the priests to say a mass for her soul. Presently she asked for a cross. An English soldier broke a stick in two and made a rough cross, which he gave her. She kissed it and put it in her bosom, weeping, calling upon God and the saints.

But the men-at-arms were growing impatient. "Come, you priests!" shouted one of them, "are you going to make us dine here?"

The bailiff of Rouen, as representing the secular power, should have now pronounced sentence of death, but he seemed afraid of delaying the soldiers, two of whom came up and seized Joan.

"Take her! take her!" he said, hurriedly, and he bade the executioner "do his duty." The bishop's trial had, after all, an illegal and informal ending.

The soldiers dragged Joan to the pile, and as she climbed it, some of her judges left their platform and rushed away, fearing to behold what they had helped to bring about. She was fastened to the stake, high up, that the flames might gain slowly upon her, and that the executioner might not be able to reach her and mercifully shorten her agony.

"Ah, Rouen!" she cried again, as she looked over the city, bright in the May sunshine—"Ah, Rouen, Rouen! I fear thou wilt have to suffer for my death!"

The executioner set fire to the pile. The confessor was by Joan's side, praying with her, comforting her so earnestly, that he took no notice of the ascending flames. It was she who saw them and bade him leave her.

"But hold up the cross," she said, "that I may see it."

Now Cauchon went to the foot of the pile, hoping perhaps that his victim might say some word of recantation. Perceiving him there, she cried aloud:

"Bishop, I die by you!"

And now the flames reached her, and she shrank from them in terror, calling for water—holy water! But as they rose and rose and wrapped her round, she seemed to draw strength from their awful contact. She still spoke. Brother Martin, standing in the heat and glare of the fire, holding the cross aloft for her comfort, heard her dying words:

"Jesus! Jesus! Mary! My voices! My voices!"

Did she hear them, those voices that had said, "Fret not thyself because of thy martyrdom; thou shalt come at last to the Kingdom of Paradise"?

"Yes," she said, "my voices were from God! My voices have not deceived me!" Then, uttering one great cry—"Jesus!" she drooped her head upon her breast, and died.

*   *   *   *   *

The common folk soon added their tale of signs and wonders to the simple and terrible truth. An English soldier, who greatly hated the Maid, had sworn to bring a faggot to her burning, and he threw it on the pile just as she gave that last cry. Suddenly he fell senseless to the earth, and when he recovered, he told how at that moment he had looked up, and had seen a white dove fly heavenward out of the fire. Others declared that they had seen the word Jesus—her dying word—written in the flames. The executioner rushed to a confessor crying that he feared to be damned, for he had burned a holy woman. But her heart would not burn, he told the priest; the rest of her body he had found consumed to ashes, but her heart was left whole and unharmed.

Many, not of the populace, were moved by her death to recognise what she had been in life.

"I would that my soul were where I believe the soul of that woman is!" exclaimed Jean Alespée, one of the judges.

"We are all lost; we have burnt a saint!" cried Tressart, a secretary of the King of England. Winchester—determined that, though she might be called a saint, there should be no relics of her—had her ashes carefully collected and thrown into the Seine.

The tidings of her death went speedily through France. They found Charles in his southern retirement, and nowise disturbed the ease of mind and body that was more to him than honour. They reached Domremy, and broke the heart of Joan's stern, loving father. Isabelle Romée lived to see her child's memory righted and her prophecies fulfilled.

✻   ✻   ✻   ✻   ✻

In June, 1455, Pope Calixtus, named a commission to inquire into the trial of Joan of Arc.

Joan's aged mother came before them, supported by her sons, and followed by a great procession of nobles, scholars, and honourable ladies. She presented the petition she had made to the Pope, and the letter whereby he granted it, and the commissioners took her aside, heard her testimony, and promised to do her justice.

And now the dead heroine was confronted with her dead judges, to their shame and her enduring honour. Messengers were sent into her country to hear the story of her innocent childhood and pure, unselfish youth. Through her whole life went the inquiry, gathering testimony from people of all ranks. The peasants whom she had loved and tended in her early girlhood, the men who had fought by her side, the women who had known and honoured her, the officers of the trial, and many who had watched her sufferings and beheld her death—all were called to speak for her now. They testified to her goodness, her purity, her single-hearted love for France, her piety, her boldness in war, and her good sense in counsel. All were for her—not one voice was raised against her. Rouen, the place of her martyrdom, became the place of her triumph.

The judges pronounced the whole trial to be polluted by wrong and calumny, and therefore null and void; finally, they proclaimed that neither Joan nor any of her kindred had incurred any blot of infamy, and freed them from every shadow of disgrace.

By order of the tribunal, this new verdict was read publicly in all the cities of France, and first at Rouen, and in the Old Market Place, where she had been cruelly burnt. This was done with great solemnity; processions were made, sermons were preached, and on the site of her martyrdom a stone cross was soon raised to her memory.

The world has no relic of Joan. Her armour, her banner, the picture of herself that she saw at Arras, have all disappeared. We possess but the record of a fair face framed in plentiful dark hair, of a strong and graceful shape, of a sweet woman's voice. And it seems—and yet, indeed, hardly is—a wonder that no worthy poem has been made in her honour. She is one of the few for whom poet and romancer can do little; for as there is nothing in her life that needs either to be hidden or adorned, we see her best in the clear and searching light of history.

VI

CATHERINE DOUGLAS

THE TRAGEDY OF JAMES I. OF SCOTS. 20TH FEBRUARY, 1437

Note.—Tradition says that Catherine Douglas, in honour of her heroic act when she barred the door with her arm against the murderers of James the First of Scots, received popularly the name of "Barlass." The name remains to her descendants, the Barlas family, in Scotland, who bear for their crest a broken arm. She married Alexander Lovell of Bolunnie.

A few stanzas from King James's lovely poem, known as *The King's Quhair*, are quoted in the course of this ballad.

I Catherine am a Douglas born, A name to all Scots dear; And Kate Barlass they've called me now Through many a waning year.

This old arm's withered now. 'T was once Most deft 'mong maidens all To rein the steed, to wing the shaft, To smite the palm-play ball.

In hall adown the close-linked dance It has shone most white and fair; It has been the rest for a true lord's head, And many a sweet babe's nursing-bed, And the bar to a King's chambère.

Ay, lasses, draw round Kate Barlass, And hark with bated breath How good King James, King Robert's son, Was foully done to death.

Through all the days of his gallant youth The princely James was pent, By his friends at first and then by his foes, In long imprisonment.

For the elder Prince, the kingdom's heir, By treason's murderous brood Was slain; and the father quaked for the child With the royal mortal blood.

I' the Bass Rock fort, by his father's care, Was his childhood's life assured; And Henry the subtle Bolingbroke,

Proud England's King, 'neath the southron yoke His youth for long years immured.

Yet in all things meet for a kingly man Himself did he approve; And the nightingale through his prison-wall Taught him both lore and love.

For once, when the bird's song drew him close To the opened window-pane, In her bowers beneath a lady stood, A light of life to his sorrowful mood, Like a lily amid the rain.

And for her sake, to the sweet bird's note, He framed a sweeter Song, More sweet than ever a poet's heart Gave yet to the English tongue.

She was a lady of royal blood; And when, past sorrow and teen He stood where still through his crownless years His Scotish realm had been, At Scone were the happy lovers crowned, A heart-wed King and Queen.

But the bird may fall from the bough of youth, And song be turned to moan, And Love's storm-cloud be the shadow of Hate, When the tempest-waves of a troubled State Are beating against a throne.

Yet well they loved; and the god of Love, Whom well the King had sung, Might find on the earth no truer hearts His lowliest swains among.

From the days when first she rode abroad With Scotish maids in her train, I Catherine Douglas won the trust Of my mistress sweet Queen Jane.

And oft she sighed, "To be born a King!" And oft along the way When she saw the homely lovers pass She has said, "Alack the day!"

Years waned, the loving and toiling years: Till England's wrong renewed Drove James, by outrage cast on his crown, To the open field of feud.

'T was when the King and his host were met At the leaguer of Roxbro' hold, The Queen o' the sudden sought his camp With a tale of dread to be told.

And she showed him a secret letter writ That spoke of treasonous strife, And how a band of his noblest lords Were sworn to take his life.

"And it may be here or it may be there, In the camp or the court," she said: "But for my sake come to your people's arms And guard your royal head."

Quoth he, "'Tis the fifteenth day of the siege, And the castle's nigh to yield." "O face your foes on your throne," she cried, "And show the power you wield; And under your Scotish people's love You shall sit as under your shield."

At the fair Queen's side I stood that day When he bade them raise the siege, And back to his Court he sped to know How the lords would meet their Liege.

But when he summoned his Parliament, The lowering brows hung round, Like clouds that circle the mountain-head Ere the first low thunders sound.

For he had tamed the nobles' lust And curbed their power and pride, And reached out an arm to right the poor Through Scotland far and wide; And marry a lordly wrong-doer By the headsman's axe had died.

'T was then upspoke Sir Robert Græme, The bold o'ermastering man: "O King, in the name of your Three Estates I set you under their ban!

"For, as your lords made oath to you Of service and fealty, Even in like wise you pledged your oath Their faithful sire to be:

"Yet all we here that are nobly sprung Have mourned dear kith and kin Since first for the Scotish Barons' curse Did your bloody rule begin."

With that he laid his hands on his King: "Is this not so, my lords?" But of all who had sworn to league with him Not one spake back to his words.

Quoth the King: "Thou speak'st but for one Estate, Nor doth it avow thy gage. Let my liege lords hale this traitor hence!" The Græme fired dark with rage: "Who works for lesser men than himself, He earns but a witless wage!"

But soon from the dungeon where he lay He won by privy plots, And forth he fled with a price on his head To the country of the Wild Scots.

And word there came from Sir Robert Græme To the King at Edinbro': "No Liege of mine thou art; but I see From this day forth alone in thee God's creature, my mortal foe.

"Through thee are my wife and children lost, My heritage and lands; And when my God shall show me a way, Thyself my mortal foe will I slay With these my proper hands."

Against the coming of Christmastide That year the King bade call I' the Black Friars' Charterhouse of Perth A solemn festival.

And we of his household rode with him In a close-ranked company; But not till the sun had sunk from his throne Did we reach the Scotish Sea.

That eve was clenched for a boding storm, 'Neath a toilsome moon, half seen; The cloud stooped low and the surf rose high; And where there was a line of the sky, Wild wings loomed dark between.

And on a rock of the black beach-side By the veiled moon dimly lit, There was something seemed to heave with life As the King drew nigh to it.

And was it only the tossing furze Or brake of the waste sea-wold? Or was it an eagle bent to the blast? When near we came, we knew it at last For a woman tattered and old.

But it seemed as though by a fire within Her writhen limbs were wrung; And as soon as the King was close to her, She stood up gaunt and strong.

'T was then the moon sailed clear of the rack On high in her hollow dome; And still as aloft with hoary crest Each clamorous wave rang home, Like fire in snow the moonlight blazed Amid the champing foam.

And the woman held his eyes with her eyes: "O King, thou art come at last; But thy wraith has haunted the Scotish Sea To my sight for four years past.

"Four years it is since first I met, 'Twixt the Duchray and the Dhu, A shape whose feet clung close in a shroud, And that shape for thine I knew.

"A year again, and on Inchkeith Isle I saw thee pass in the breeze, With the cerecloth risen above thy feet And wound about thy knees.

"And yet a year, in the Links of Forth, As a wanderer without rest, Thou cam'st with both thine arms i' the shroud That clung high up thy breast.

"And in this hour I find thee here, And well mine eyes may note That the winding-sheet hath passed thy breast And risen around thy throat.

"And when I meet thee again, O King, That of death hast such sore drouth, Except thou turn again on this shore, The winding-sheet shall have moved once more And covered thine eyes and mouth.

"O King, whom poor men bless for their King, Of thy fate be not so fain; But these my words for God's message take, And turn thy steed, O King, for her sake Who rides beside thy rein!"

While the woman spoke, the King's horse reared As if it would breast the sea, And the Queen turned pale as she heard on the gale The voice die dolorously.

When the woman ceased, the steed was still, But the King gazed on her yet, And in silence save for the wail of the sea His eyes and her eyes met.

At last he said: "God's ways are His own; Man is but shadow and dust. Last night I prayed by His altar-stone; To-night I wend to the Feast of His Son; And in Him I set my trust.

"I have held my people in sacred charge, And have not feared the sting Of proud men's hate, to His will resign'd Who has but one same death for a hind And one same death for a King.

"And if God in His wisdom have brought close The day when I must die, That day by water or fire or air My feet shall fall in the destined snare Wherever my road may lie.

"What man can say but the Fiend hath set Thy sorcery on my path, My heart with the fear of death to fill, And turn me against God's very will To sink in His burning wrath?"

The woman stood as the train rode past, And moved nor limb nor eye; And when we were shipped, we saw her there Still standing against the sky.

As the ship made way, the moon once more Sank slow in her rising pall; And I thought of the shrouded wraith of the King, And I said, "The Heavens know all."

And now, ye lasses, must ye hear How my name is Kate Barlass: But a little thing, when all the tale Is told of the weary mass Of crime and woe which in Scotland's realm God's will let come to pass.

'T was in the Charterhouse of Perth That the King and all his Court Were met, the Christmas Feast being done, For solace and disport.

'T was a wind-wild eve in February, And against the casement-pane The branches smote like summoning hands And muttered the driving rain.

And when the wind swooped over the lift And made the whole heaven frown, It seemed a grip was laid on the walls To tug the housetop down.

And the Queen was there, more stately fair Than a lily in garden set; And the King was loth to stir from her side; For as on the day when she was his bride, Even so he loved her yet.

And the Earl of Athole, the King's false friend, Sat with him at the board; And Robert Stuart the chamberlain Who had sold his sovereign Lord.

Yet the traitor Christopher Chaumber there Would fain have told him all, And vainly four times that night he strove To reach the King through the hall.

But the wine is bright at the goblet's brim Though the poison lurk beneath; And the apples still are red on the tree Within whose shade may the adder be That shall turn thy life to death.

There was a knight of the King's fast friends Whom he called the King of Love; And to such bright cheer and courtesy That name might best behove.

And the King and Queen both loved him well For his gentle knightliness; And with him the King, as that eve wore on, Was playing at the chess.

And the King said (for he thought to jest And soothe the Queen thereby), "In a book 'tis writ that this same year A King shall in Scotland die.

"And I have pondered the matter o'er, And this have I found, Sir Hugh, There are but two Kings on Scotish ground, And those Kings are I and you.

"And I have a wife and a newborn heir, And you are yourself alone; So stand you stark at my side with me To guard our double throne."

"For here sit I and my wife and child, As well your heart shall approve, In full surrender and soothfastness, Beneath your Kingdom of Love."

And the Knight laughed, and the Queen, too, smiled; But I knew her heavy thought, And I strove to find in the good King's jest What cheer might thence be wrought.

And I said, "My Liege, for the Queen's dear love Now sing the song that of old You made, when a captive Prince you lay, And the nightingale sang sweet on the spray, In Windsor's castle-hold."

Then he smiled the smile I knew so well When he thought to please the Queen; The smile which under all bitter frowns Of hate that rose between, For ever dwelt at the poet's heart Like the bird of love unseen.

And he kissed her hand and took his harp, And the music sweetly rang; And when the song burst forth, it seemed 'T was the nightingale that sang.

"*Worship, ye lovers, on this May: Of bliss your kalends are begun: Sing with us, Away, Winter, away! Come, Summer, the sweet season and sun! Awake for shame, your heaven is won, And amorously your heads lift all: Thank Love, that you to his grace doth call!"*

But when he bent to the Queen, and sang The speech whose praise was hers, It seemed his voice was the voice of the Spring And the voice of the bygone years.

"The fairest and the freshest flower That ever I saw before that hour, The which o' the sudden made to start The blood of my body to my heart.

*   *   *   *   *

Ah sweet, are ye a worldly creature Or heavenly thing in form of nature?"

And the song was long, and richly stored With wonder and beauteous things; And the harp was tuned to every change Of minstrel ministerings; But when he spoke of the Queen at the last, Its strings were his own heart-strings.

"Unworthy but only of her grace, Upon Love's rock that's easy and sure, In guerdon of all my love's space She took me her humble creäture. Thus fell my blissful aventure In youth of love that from day to day Flowereth aye new, and further, I say.

"To reck all the circumstance As it happed when lessen gan my sore, Of my rancor and woeful chance, It were too long—I have done therefor. And of this flower I say no more But unto my help her heart hath tended And even from death her man defended."

"Ay, even from death," to myself I said; For I thought of the day when she Had borne him the news, at Roxbro' siege, Of the fell confederacy.

But death even then took aim as he sang With an arrow deadly bright; And the grinning skull lurked grimly aloof, And the wings were spread far over the roof More dark than the winter night.

Yet truly along the amorous song Of Love's high pomp and state, There were words of Fortune's trackless doom And the dreadful face of Fate.

And oft have I heard again in dreams The voice of dire appeal In which the King sang of the pit That is under Fortune's wheel.

"*And under the wheel beheld I there An ugly Pit as deep as hell, That to behold I quaked for fear: And this I heard, that who therein fell Came no more up, tidings to tell: Whereat, astound of the fearful sight, I wist not what to do for fright.*"

And oft has my thought called up again These words of the changeful song: "*Wist thou thy pain and thy travàil To come, well might'st thou weep and wail!*" And our wail, O God! is long.

But the song's end was all of his love; And well his heart was grac'd With her smiling lips and her tear-bright eyes As his arm went round her waist.

And on the swell of her long fair throat Close clung the necklet-chain As he bent her pearl-tir'd head aside, And in the warmth of his love and pride He kissed her lips full fain.

And her true face was a rosy red, The very red of the rose That, couched on the happy garden-bed, In the summer sunlight glows.

And all the wondrous things of love That sang so sweet through the song Were in the look that met in their eyes, And the look was deep and long.

'T was then a knock came at the outer gate, And the usher sought the King. "The woman you met by the Scotish Sea, My Liege, would tell you a thing; And she says that her present need for speech Will bear no gainsaying."

And the King said: "The hour is late; To-morrow will serve, I ween." Then he charged the usher strictly, and said: "No word of this to the Queen."

But the usher came again to the King. "Shall I call her back?" quoth he: "For as she went on her way, she cried, 'Woe! Woe! then the thing must be!'"

And the King paused, but he did not speak. Then he called for the Voidee-cup: And as we heard the twelfth hour strike, There by true lips and false lips alike Was the draught of trust drained up.

So with reverence meet to King and Queen To bed went all from the board; And the last to leave the courtly train Was Robert Stuart the chamberlain Who had sold his sovereign lord.

And all the locks of the chamber-door Had the traitor riven and brast; And that Fate might win sure way from afar, He had drawn out every bolt and bar That made the entrance fast.

And now at midnight he stole his way To the moat of the outer wall, And laid strong hurdles closely across Where the traitors' tread should fall.

But we that were the Queen's bower-maids Alone were left behind; And with heed we drew the curtains close Against the winter wind.

And now that all was still through the hall, More clearly we heard the rain That clamoured ever against the glass And the boughs that beat on the pane

But the fire was bright in the ingle-nook, And through empty space around The shadows cast on the arras'd wall 'Mid the pictured kings stood sudden and tall Like spectres sprung from the ground.

And the bed was dight in a deep alcove; And as he stood by the fire The King was still in talk with the Queen While he doffed his goodly attire.

And the song had brought the image back Of many a bygone year; And many a loving word they said With hand in hand and head laid to head; And none of us went anear.

But Love was weeping outside the house, A child in the piteous rain; And as he watched the arrow of Death, He wailed for his own shafts close in the sheath That never should fly again.

And now beneath the window arose A wild voice suddenly: And the King reared straight, but the Queen fell back As for bitter dule to dree; And all of us knew the woman's voice Who spoke by the Scotish Sea.

"O King," she cried, "in an evil hour They drove me from thy gate; And yet my voice must rise to thine ears; But alas! it comes too late!

"Last night at mid-watch, by Aberdour, When the moon was dead in the skies, O King, in a death-light of thine own I saw thy shape arise.

"And in full season, as erst I said, The doom had gained its growth; And the shroud had risen above thy neck And covered thine eyes and mouth.

"And no moon woke, but the pale dawn broke, And still thy soul stood there; And I thought its silence cried to my soul As the first rays crowned its hair.

"Since then have I journeyed fast and fain In very despite of Fate, Lest Hope might still be found in God's will: But they drove me from thy gate.

"For every man on God's ground, O King, His death grows up from his birth In the shadow-plant perpetually; And thine towers high, a black yew-tree, O'er the Charterhouse of Perth!"

That room was built far out from the house; And none but we in the room Might hear the voice that rose beneath, Nor the tread of the coming doom.

For now there came a torchlight-glare, And a clang of arms there came; And not a soul in that space but thought Of the foe Sir Robert Græme.

Yea, from the country of the Wild Scots, O'er mountain, valley, and glen, He had brought with him in murderous league Three hundred armèd men.

The King knew all in an instant's flash, And like a King did he stand; But there was no armour in all the room, Nor weapon lay to his hand.

And all we women flew to the door And thought to have made it fast; But the bolts were gone and the bars were gone And the locks were riven and brast.

And he caught the pale pale Queen in his arms As the iron footsteps fell, Then loosed her, standing alone, and said, "Our bliss was our farewell!"

And 'twixt his lips he murmured a prayer, And he crossed his brow and breast; And proudly in royal hardihood Even so with folded arms he stood— The prize of the bloody quest.

Then on me leaped the Queen like a deer: "O Catherine, help!" she cried. And low at his feet we clasped his knees Together side by side. "Oh! even a King, for his people's sake, From treasonous death must hide!"

"For *her* sake most!" I cried, and I marked The pang that my words could wring. And the iron tongs from the chimney-nook I snatched and held to the King: "Wrench up the plank! and the vault beneath Shall yield safe harbouring."

With brows low-bent, from my eager hand The heavy heft did he take; And the plank at his feet he wrenched and tore; And as he frowned through the open floor, Again I said, "For her sake!"

Then he cried to the Queen, "God's will be done!" For her hands were clasped in prayer. And down he sprang to the inner crypt; And straight we closed the plank he had ripp'd And toiled to smoothe it fair.

(Alas! in that vault a gap once was Wherethro' the King might have fled; But three days since close-walled had it been By his will; for the ball would roll therein When without at the palm he play'd.)

Then the Queen cried, "Catherine, keep the door, And I to this will suffice!" At her word I rose all dazed to my feet, And my heart was fire and ice.

And louder ever the voices grew, And the tramp of men in mail; Until to my brain it seemed to be As though I tossed on a ship at sea In the teeth of a crashing gale.

Then back I flew to the rest; and hard We strove with sinews knit To force the table against the door But we might not compass it.

Then my wild gaze sped far down the hall To the place of the hearthstone-sill; And the Queen bent ever above the floor, For the plank was rising still.

And now the rush was heard on the stair, And "God, what help?" was our cry. And was I frenzied or was I bold? I looked at each empty stanchion-hold, And no bar but my arm had I!

Like iron felt my arm, as through The staple I made it pass: Alack! it was flesh and bone—no more! 'T was Catherine Douglas sprang to the door, But I fell back Kate Barlass.

With that they all thronged into the hall, Half dim to my failing ken; And the space that was but a void before Was a crowd of wrathful men.

Behind the door I had fall'n and lay, Yet my sense was widely aware, And for all the pain of my shattered arm I never fainted there.

Even as I fell, my eyes were cast Where the King leaped down to the pit; And lo! the plank was smooth in its place, And the Queen stood far from it.

And under the litters and through the bed And within the presses all The traitors sought for the King, and pierced The arras around the wall.

And through the chamber they ramped and stormed Like lions loose in the lair, And scarce could trust to their very eyes— For behold! no King was there.

Then one of them seized the Queen, and cried, "Now tells us, where is thy lord?" And he held the sharp point over her heart: She drooped not her eyes nor did she start, But she answered never a word.

Then the sword half pierced the true true breast: But it was the Græme's own son Cried, "This is a woman—we seek a man!" And away from her girdle-zone He struck the point of the murderous steel; And that foul deed was not done.

And forth flowed all the throng like a sea, And 't was empty space once more; And my eyes sought out the wounded Queen As I lay behind the door.

And I said: "Dear Lady, leave me here, For I cannot help you now; But fly while you may, and none shall reck Of my place here lying low."

And she said, "My Catherine, God help thee!" Then she looked to the distant floor, And clasping her hands, "O God help _him_," She sobbed, "for we can no more!"

But God He knows what help may mean, If it mean to live or to die; And what sore sorrow and mighty moan On earth it may cost ere yet a throne Be filled in His house on high.

And now the ladies fled with the Queen; And through the open door The night-wind wailed round the empty room And the rushes shook on the floor.

And the bed drooped low in the dark recess Whence the arras was rent away; And the firelight still shone over the space Where our hidden secret lay.

And the rain had ceased, and the moonbeams lit The window high in the wall— Bright beams that on the plank that I knew Through the painted pane did fall And gleamed with the splendour of Scotland's crown And shield armorial.

But then a great wind swept up the skies, And the climbing moon fell back; And the royal blazon fled from the floor, And naught remained on its track; And high in the darkened window-pane The shield and the crown were black.

And what I say next I partly saw And partly I heard in sooth, And partly since from the murderers' lips The torture wrung the truth.

For now again came the armèd tread, And fast through the hall it fell; But the throng was less: and ere I saw, By the voice without I could tell That Robert Stuart had come with them Who knew that chamber well.

And over the space the Græme strode dark With his mantle round him flung; And in his eye was a flaming light But not a word on his tongue.

And Stuart held a torch to the floor, And he found the thing he sought; And they slashed the plank away with their swords And O God! I fainted not!

And the traitor held his torch in the gap, All smoking and smouldering; And through the vapour and fire, beneath In the dark crypt's narrow ring, With a shout that pealed to the room's high roof They saw their naked King.

Half naked he stood, but stood as one Who yet could do and dare; With the crown, the King was stript away— The Knight was reft of his battle-array— But still the Man was there.

From the rout then stepped a villain forth— Sir John Hall was his name: With a knife unsheathed he leapt to the vault Beneath the torchlight-flame.

Of his person and stature was the King A man right manly strong, And mightily by the shoulderblades His foe to his feet he flung.

Then the traitor's brother, Sir Thomas Hall, Sprang down to work his worst; And the King caught the second man by the neck And flung him above the first.

And he smote and trampled them under him; And a long month thence they bare All black their throats with the grip of his hands When the hangman's hand came there.

And sore he strove to have had their knives, But the sharp blades gashed his hands. Oh James! so armed, thou hadst battled there Till help had come of thy bands; And oh! once more thou hadst held our throne And ruled thy Scotish lands!

But while the King o'er his foes still raged With a heart that naught could tame, Another man sprange down to the crypt; And with his sword in his hand hard-gripp'd, There stood Sir Robert Græme.

(Now shame on the recreant traitor's heart Who durst not face his King Till the body unarmed was wearied out With two-fold combating!

Ah! well might the people sing and say, As oft ye have heard aright: "*O Robert Græme, O Robert Græme, Who slew our King, God give thee shame!*" For he slew him not as a knight.)

And the naked King turned round at bay, But his strength had passed the goal, And he could but gasp: "Mine hour is come; But oh! to succour thine own soul's doom, Let a priest now shrive my soul!"

And the traitor looked on the King's spent strength And said: "Have I kept my word? Yea, King, the mortal pledge that I gave? No black friar's shrift thy soul shall have, But the shrift of this red sword!"

With that he smote his King through the breast; And all they three in the pen Fell on him and stabbed and stabbed him there Like merciless murderous men

Yet seemed it now that Sir Robert Græme, Ere the King's last breath was o'er, Turned sick at heart with the deadly sight And would have done no more.

But a cry came from the troop above: "If him thou do not slay, The price of his life that thou dost spare Thy forfeit life shall pay!"

O God! what more did I hear or see, Or how should I tell the rest? But there at length our King lay slain With sixteen wounds in his breast.

O God! and now did a bell boom forth, And the murderers turned and fled; Too late, too late, O God, did it sound! And I heard the true men mustering round, And the cries and the coming tread.

But ere they came, to the black death-gap Somewise did I creep and steal; And lo! or ever I swooned away, Through the dusk I saw where the white face lay In the Pit of Fortune's Wheel.

And now, ye Scotish maids who have heard Dread things of the days grown old— Even at the last, of true Queen Jane May somewhat yet be told, And how she dealt for her dear Lord's sake Dire vengeance manifold.

'T was in the Charterhouse of Perth, In the fair-lit Death-chapelle, That the slain King's corpse on bier was laid With chaunt and requiem-knell.

And all with royal wealth of balm Was the body purified; And none could trace on the brow and lips The death that he had died.

In his robes of state he lay asleep With orb and sceptre in hand; And by the crown he wore on his throne Was his kingly forehead spann'd.

And, girls, 't was a sweet sad thing to see How the curling golden hair, As in the day of the poet's youth, From the King's crown clustered there.

And if all had come to pass in the brain That throbbed beneath those curls, Then Scots had said in the days to come That this their soil was a different home And a different Scotland, girls!

And the Queen sat by him night and days And oft she knelt in prayer, All wan and pale in the widow's veil That shrouded her shining hair.

And I had got good help of my hurt: And only to me some sign She made; and save the priests that were there No face would she see but mine.

And the month of March wore on apace; And now fresh couriers fared Still from the country of the Wild Scots With news of the traitors snared.

And still, as I told her day by day, Her pallor changed to sight, And the frost grew to a furnace-flame That burnt her visage white.

And evermore as I brought her word, She bent to her dead King James, And in the cold ear with fire-drawn breath She spoke the traitors' names.

But when the name of Sir Robert Græme Was the one she had to give, I ran to hold her up from the floor; For the froth was on her lips, and sore I feared that she could not live.

And the month of March wore nigh to its end, And still was the death-pall spread; For she would not bury her slaughtered lord Till his slayers all were dead.

And now of their dooms dread tidings came, And of torments fierce and dire; And naught she spake—she had ceased to speak— But her eyes were a soul on fire.

But when I told her the bitter end Of the stern and just award, She leaned o'er the bier, and thrice three times She kissed the lips of her lord.

And then she said, "My King, they are dead!" And she knelt on the chapel floor, And whispered low with a strange proud smile, "James, James, they suffered more!"

Last she stood up to her queenly height, But she shook like an autumn leaf, As though the fire wherein she burned Then left her body, and all were turned To winter of life-long grief.

And "O James!" she said, "My James!" she said, "Alas for the woeful thing, That a poet true and a friend of man, In desperate days of bale and ban, Should needs be born a King!"

VII

LADY JANE GREY

"Seventeen—and knew eight languages—in music
Peerless—her needle perfect, and her learning Beyond the
Churchmen; yet so meek, so modest, So wife-like humble to the
trivial boy Mismatched with her for policy! I have heard She
would not take a last farewell of him; She feared it might unman
him for his end. She could not be unmanned—no, nor
outwoman'd. Seventeen—a rose of grace! Girl never breathed to
rival such a rose; Rose never blew that equalled such a bud."

—Tennyson.

When the hapless daughter of Dudley, Duke of
Northumberland, offered up her fair young life upon the scaffold
at Tower Hill she was still in her "teens"—with the simplicity
and freshness of girlhood upon her. There is a tender and pathetic
beauty about the tragic tale which no repetition can wholly dim
or wear off.

The reader needs not to be told that she was the eldest
daughter of Henry Grey, third Marquis of Dorset. She was allied
with royal blood, her mother being Frances the eldest daughter of
Charles Brandon, Duke of Suffolk, and Mary Tudor, second
daughter of Henry VII. She came also of royal stock on the
father's side.

It is a curious fact that the date of the birth of this lady is
not exactly known; but, according to Fuller, it took place in
1536, at her father's stately mansion, of Bradgate, near Leicester.
She was the eldest of three daughters, Jane, Katherine and Mary.
At a very early age her budding gifts gave abundant promise of a
fair womanhood; so serene her temper and so remarkable her love
of knowledge. She was fortunate in living at a time when the
education of women was as comprehensive and exact as that of
men; and her father provided her with two learned tutors in his
two chaplains, Thomas Harding and John Aylmer. To the latter

she seems to have been more particularly given in charge; and the teacher being as zealous as the pupil was diligent, Lady Jane soon gained a thorough acquaintance with Latin and Greek, and also some degree of proficiency in Hebrew, Arabic, Chaldaic, French and Italian.

These grave and serious studies were relieved by a cultivation of the graces. Her voice was melodious, and she sang with much skill and expression; she also played on various musical instruments. Her needle-work and embroidery excited the admiration of her contemporaries; she acquired a knowledge of the medical properties of herbs; dainty dishes, preserves, and "sweet waters" she concocted with dexterous hand; her calligraphy was a marvel of ease and elegance; in this last-named art she was instructed by the erudite Roger Ascham, who was one of its most famous professors.

Thus it happened that even in her early girlhood she surpassed in general scholarship her equals in age. But her tutors did not forget the spiritual side of her education, and she was well grounded in the dogmas of the Church as well as in the truths and lessons embodied in the life and teaching of her Lord.

After the death of Henry VIII. Lady Jane went to reside with the widowed Queen, Katherine Parr, at Chelsea; and when that lady married Lord Seymour of Dudley, she accompanied them to Hanworth, in Middlesex, a palace which Henry VIII. had bestowed upon Queen Katherine in dower. The Queen did not long survive her second nuptials, but died at Dudley Castle, September 5, 1548, in the thirty-sixth year of her age. Lady Jane acted as chief mourner at the funeral.

It was soon after this event that Lady Jane addressed the following letter to the Lord High Admiral. As the composition of a girl of twelve it shows no ordinary promise:—

October 1, 1548.

My duty to your lordship, in most humble wise remembered, with no less thanks for the gentle letters which I received from you. Thinking myself so much bound to your lordship for your great goodness towards me from time to time, that I cannot by any means be able to recompense the least part thereof, I purposed to write a few rude lines unto your lordship, rather as a token to show how much worthier I think your lordship's goodness than to give worthy thanks for the same; and these my letters shall be to testify unto you that, like as you have become towards me a loving and kind father, so I shall be always most ready to obey your godly monitions and good instructions, as becometh one upon whom you have heaped so many benefits. And thus, fearing lest I should trouble your lordship too much, I must humbly take my leave of your good lordship.

Your humble servant during my life, Jane Grey.

It is not impossible that at Bradgate Lady Jane may have regretted the indulgent ease and splendid hospitality of Dudley Castle. Her parents acted upon the maxim that to spare the rod is to spoil the child; and notwithstanding her amiability and honourable diligence, subjected her to a very severe discipline. She was rigorously punished for the slightest defect in her behaviour or the most trivial failure in her studies. Her parents taught her to fear, rather than to love, them; and insisted upon reverence, rather than affection, as the duty of children. It is no wonder, therefore, that from the austere brow and unsympathetic voice she turned with ever-increasing delight towards that secret spirit of knowledge which has only smiles for its votaries.

In the pages of the wise she met with divine words of encouragement and consolation; they soothed her sorrows, they taught her the heroism of endurance, they lifted her into that serene realm where dwelt the Immortals—the glorious minds of old. "Thus," says she, "my book hath been so much my pleasure, and bringeth daily to me more and more pleasure, that in respect of it all other pleasures in very deed be but trifles and troubles unto me."

From an interesting passage in Roger Ascham's "Schoolmaster," we can form some idea of the melancholy girlhood of this daughter of a royal race. Ascham visited Bradgate in the summer of 1550 on his way to London. He found, on his arrival, the stately mansion deserted; the Lord and Lady, with all their household, were hunting merrily in the park to the music of horn and hound. Making his way through the deserted chambers, he came at length upon a secluded apartment, where the fair Lady Jane was calmly studying the pages of Plato's immortal "Phædon" in the original Greek. Surprised and delighted by a spectacle so unusual, the worthy scholar, after the usual salutations, inquired why she had not accompanied the gay lords and ladies in the park, to enjoy the pastime of the chase.

"I wis," she replied, smiling, "all their sport in the park is but a shadow to that pleasure that I find in Plato. Alas! good folk, they never felt what true pleasure meant."

"And how came you, madam," quoth he, "to this deep knowledge of pleasure? And what did chiefly allure you unto it, seeing not many women, but very few men, have attained thereunto?"

"I will tell you," quoth she, "and tell you a truth which, perchance, ye will marvel at. One of the greatest benefits that ever God gave me is that He sent me so sharp and severe parents and so gentle a schoolmaster. For when I am in presence either of father or mother, whether I speak, keep silence, sit, stand, or go, eat, drink, be merry or sad, be sewing, playing, dancing or doing anything else, I must do it, as it were, in such weight, measure and number, even so perfectly as God made the world, or else I am so sharply taunted, so cruelly threatened, yea, presently, sometimes with pinches, nips and bobs, and other ways which I will not name for the honour I bear them, so without reason misordered, that I think myself in hell till time come that I must go to Mr. Aylmer; who teacheth me so gently, so pleasantly, with such fair allurements to learning, that I think all the time nothing whiles I am with him. And when I am called from him, I fall on weeping, because, whatever I do else but learning is full of grief, trouble, fear and whole misliking unto me."

Ascham did not see her again after this memorable interview. "I remember this talk gladly," he wrote, "both because it is so worthy of memory and because also it was the last talk that ever I had and the last time that ever I saw that noble and worthy lady."

In his letters to his learned friends, however, he frequently commented on the sweetness of her character and the depth of her erudition. He spoke of Lady Mildred Cooke and the Lady Jane Grey as the two most learned women in England; and summed up his praises of the latter in the remark that "however illustrious she was by her fortune and royal extraction, this bore no proportion to the accomplishments of her mind, adorned with the doctrine of Plato and the eloquence of Demosthenes."

Her illustrious rank, her piety and her erudition necessarily made the Lady Jane an object of special interest to the leaders of the Reformed Church in England and on the continent. The learned Martin Bruce, whom Edward VI. had appointed to the chair of divinity at the University of Cambridge, watched over her with prayerful anxiety. Bullinger, a minister of Zurich, corresponded with her frequently, encouraging her in the practice of every virtue. Under the direction and counsel of these and other divines she pursued her theological studies with great success, so as to be able to defend and maintain the creed she had adopted, and give abundant reason for the faith that was in her.

The Marquis of Dorset, in October, 1551, was raised to the dukedom of Suffolk; and on the same day the subtle and ambitious intriguer, John Dudley, Earl of Warwick, who was to exercise so malignant an influence on his daughter's destiny, was created Duke of Northumberland.

The Lady Jane was then removed to the metropolis, residing with her family at her father's town house, in Suffolk Place. She necessarily shared in the festivities of the court; but she would seem to have been distinguished always by a remarkable plainness of apparel; in this obeying the impulse of her simplicity of taste, supported and confirmed by the advice of Bullinger and Aylmer.

On one occasion the Princess Mary presented her with a sumptuous robe, which she was desired to wear in recognition of the donor's generosity. "Nay," she replied, "that were a shame, to follow my Lady Mary, who leaveth God's word, and leave my

Lady Elizabeth who followeth God's word." A speech which the Lady Mary doubtless remembered.

Early in 1553, men clearly saw that the life and reign of Edward VI. were drawing to an abrupt termination. His legitimate successor was his elder sister Mary; but her morose temper and bigoted attachment to the old Church had filled the minds of the Reformers with anxiety. Her unpopularity, and the dangers to the Reformed Church to be apprehended from her accession, led Dudley, Duke of Northumberland, to conceive an audacious design. He resolved to raise his son to the throne. But for this purpose it was necessary to ally him to the blood-royal, and he therefore planned a marriage between his young son, Lord Guilford Dudley, and Lady Jane Grey.

There were such elements of fitness in the match that on neither side was any obstruction thrown; and in June 1553 the bridal ceremony took place at the Duke of Northumberland's palace in the Strand. The Duke then obtained from King Edward, by an appeal to his zeal for the Church, letters-patent excluding Mary and Elizabeth from the succession and declaring Lady Jane Grey heir to the throne.

A few days afterwards the young king died; and on the evening of the 9th of July, the Duke of Northumberland, accompanied by the Marquis of Northampton, the Earls of Arundel, Huntingdon and Pembroke, appeared before the young bride in her quiet chamber at Northumberland House, and urged her acceptance of a crown which was fated to become, for her, a crown of thorns.

"How I was beside myself," she afterwards wrote, "how I was beside myself, stupefied and troubled, I will leave it to those lords who were present to testify, who saw me overcome by sudden and unexpected grief, fall on the ground, weeping very bitterly; and then declaring to them my insufficiency, I greatly bewailed myself for the death of so noble a Prince, and at the same time turned myself to God, humbly praying and beseeching Him that if what was given to me was *rightly and lawfully* mine, His divine Majesty would grant *me* such grace and spirit that I might govern it to His glory and service and to the advantage of this realm."

Her prudent reluctance, however, was overruled. History records the brief twelve days' pageant of her reign.

On the 19th of July her opponent, Mary entered London in triumph.

"Great was the rejoicing," says a contemporary; so great that the like of it had never been seen by any living. The number of caps that were flung into the air at the proclamation could not be told. The Earl of Pembroke cast among the crowd a liberal largess. Bonfires blazed in every street; and what with shouting and crying of the people, and ringing of bells, there could no one man hear what another said.

Lady Jane was at first confined in the house of one Partridge, a warder of the Tower. Thence, after she and her husband had been tried for high treason and found guilty, they were removed to the Tower. During her captivity she occasionally amused herself with the graceful pursuits of her earlier and happier years, engraving on the walls of her prison, with a pin, some Latin distich, which turned into English read:

"Believe not, man, in care's despite, That thou from others' ills art free The *cross* that now *I* suffer might To-morrow haply fall on *thee*"

"Endless all malice, if our God is nigh: Fruitless all pains, if He His help deny, Patient I pass these gloomy hours away, And wait the morning of eternal day."

Her execution was fixed for the 12th of February 1554. On the night preceding she wrote a few sentences of advice to her sister on the blank leaf of a New Testament. To her father she addressed the following beautiful letter, in which filial reverence softens and subdues the exhortations of a dying saint:

The Lord comfort Your Grace, and that in His Word, wherein all creatures only are to be comforted; and though it hath pleased God to take away two of your children, yet think not, I most humbly beseech Your Grace, that you have lost them; but trust that we, by leaving this mortal life, have won an immortal life. And I, for my part, as I have honoured Your Grace in this life, will pray for you in another life.—Your Grace's humble daughter,

Jane Dudley.

The stern Lieutenant of the Tower, Sir John Brydges, had been vanquished by the gentle graces of his prisoner and he sought from her some memorial in writing. In a manual of manuscript prayers she wrote a few sentences of farewell:

Forasmuch as you have desired so simple a woman to write in so worthy a book, good Master Lieutenant, therefore I shall, as a friend, desire you, and as a Christian require you, to call upon God to incline your heart to His laws, to quicken you in His way, and not to take the word of truth utterly out of your mouth. Live still to die, that by death you may purchase eternal life, and remember how Methuselah, who, as we read in the Scriptures, was the longest liver that was of a man, died at the last; for, as the Preacher saith, there is a time to be born and a time to die; and the day of death is better than the day of our birth.—Yours, as the Lord knoweth, as a friend,

Jane Dudley.

Mary and her advisers had originally intended that both Lady Jane and her husband should be executed together on Tower Hill; but reflection convinced them that the spectacle of so comely and youthful a pair suffering for what was rather the crime of others than their own, might powerfully awaken the sympathies of the multitude, and produce a revulsion of feeling. It was ordered, therefore, that Lady Jane should suffer within the precincts of the Tower.

The fatal morning came. The young husband—still a bridegroom and a lover—had obtained permission to bid her a last farewell; but she refused to see him, apprehensive that so bitter a parting might overwhelm them, and deprive them of the courage needful to face death with calmness. She sent him, however, many loving messages, reminding him how brief would be their separation, and how quickly they would meet in a brighter and better world.

In going to his death on Tower Hill, he passed beneath the window of her cell; so that they had an opportunity of exchanging a farewell look. He behaved on the scaffold with calm intrepidity. After spending a brief space in silent devotion, he requested the prayers of the spectators, and, laying his head upon the block, gave the fatal signal. At one blow his head was severed from his body.

The scaffold on which the girl-queen was to close her stainless career had been erected on the green opposite the White Tower. As soon as her husband was dead the officers announced that the sheriffs waited to attend her thither. And when she had gone down and been delivered into their hands, the bystanders noted in her "a countenance so gravely settled and with all modest and comely resolution, that not the least symptom either of fear or grief could be perceived either in her speech or motions; she was like one going to be united to her heart's best and longest beloved."

So, like a martyr, crowned with glory, she went unto her death. Her serene composure was scarcely shaken when, through an unfortunate misunderstanding of the officer in command, she met on her way her husband's headless trunk being borne to its last resting-place.

"Oh Guilford! Guilford!" she exclaimed; "the antepast is not so bitter that you have tasted, and that I shall soon taste, as to make my flesh tremble; it is nothing compared to the feast that you and I shall this day partake of in heaven." This thought renewed her strength and sustained and consoled, we might almost believe, by ministering angels, she proceeded to the scaffold with as much grace and dignity as if it were a wedding banquet that awaited her.

She was conducted by Sir John Brydges, the Lieutenant of the Tower, and attended by her two waiting-women, Mrs. Elizabeth Tylney and Mrs. Ellen. While these wept and sobbed bitterly, her eyes were dry, and her countenance shone with the light of a sure and certain hope. She read earnestly her manual of prayers. On reaching the place of execution she saluted the lords and gentlemen present with unshaken composure and infinite grace. No minister of her own Church had been allowed to attend her, and she did not care to accept the services of Feckenham, Queen Mary's confessor. She was not indifferent, however, to his respectful sympathy and when bidding him farewell, she said:

"Go now; God grant you all your desires, and accept my own warm thanks for your attentions to me; although, indeed, those attentions have tried me more than death could now terrify me."

To the spectators she addressed a few gentle words, in admirable keeping with the gentle tenor of her life.

"Good people," she exclaimed, "I am come hither to die, and by law I am condemned to the same. My offence to the Queen's Highness was only in consent to the device of others, which now is deemed treason; but it was never my seeking, but by counsel of those who should seem to have further understanding of things than I, who knew little of the law, and much less of the titles to the Crown. I pray you all, good Christian people, to bear me witness that I die a true Christian woman, and that I look to be saved by none other means but only by the mercy of God, in the merits of the blood of His only son, Jesus Christ; and I confess, when I did know the word of God, I neglected the same, loved myself and the world, and therefore this plague or punishment is happily and worthily happened unto me for my sins; and yet I thank God of His goodness, that He hath thus given me a time and respite to repent. And now, good people, while I am alive, I pray you to assist me with your prayers."

She knelt to her devotions, and turning to Feckenham, inquired whether she should repeat the Miserere psalm (the fifty-first, "Have mercy upon me, O Lord").

He replied in the affirmative; and she said it with great earnestness from beginning to end. Rising from her knees, she began to prepare herself for the headsman and pulling off her gloves, gave them and her handkerchief to Mistress Tylney. The manual of prayers, in which she had written at the desire of the Lieutenant, she handed to Thomas Brydges, his brother. When she was unfastening her robe, the executioner would have assisted her, but she motioned him aside, and accepted the last offices of her waiting-women, who then gave her a white handkerchief with which to bandage her eyes.

Throwing himself at her feet, the headsman humbly craved her forgiveness, which she willingly granted. He then requested her to stand upon the straw, and in complying with his direction she for the first time saw the fatal block. Her composure remained unshaken; she simply entreated the executioner to dispatch her quickly. Again kneeling she asked him:

"Will you take it off before I lay me down?"

"No, madam," he replied.

She bound the handkerchief round her eyes, and feeling for the block, exclaimed,

"What shall I do? Where is it?"

Being guided to it by one of the bystanders, she laid her head down, exclaiming, in an audible voice:

"Lord, into thy hands I commend my spirit."

In an instant the axe fell, and the tragedy was consummated. An involuntary groan from the assembled multitude seemed to acknowledge that vengeance had been satisfied, but justice outraged.

Lady Jane—or Queen Jane, as she should more properly be called—was little more than seventeen years old when she thus fell a victim to Mary's jealous fears and hate. She had hardly entered upon womanhood, and the promise of her young life had had no time to ripen into fruition. We may well believe, however, that she would not have disappointed the hopes which that promise had awakened. Her heroic death showed how well she had profited by the lessons she had imbibed in her early years.

There was no affectation, no exaggeration, in her conduct upon the scaffold; but she bore herself with serene dignity and with true courage. It was worthy of her life—which, brief as an unhappy fortune made it, was full of beauty, full of calmness, and truth, and elevation and modest piety. The impression which it made upon her contemporaries, an impression taken up and retained by posterity, is visible in the fact to this hour we speak of her as she was in her sweet simple maidenhood—we pass over her married name and her regal title, and love to honour her, not as Lady Jane Dudley, or Queen Jane, but as Lady Jane Grey.

VIII

POCAHONTAS

In his younger days Powhatan had been a great warrior. He was the chief, or *werowance*, of eight tribes. Through conquest his dominions had been extended until they reached from the James River to the Potomac, from the sea to the falls in the rivers, and included thirty of the forty tribes in Virginia. It is estimated that his subjects numbered eight thousand. The name of his nation and the Indian name of the James River was Powhatan. His enemies were two neighbouring confederacies, the Mannahoacs, between the Rappahannock and York rivers, and the Monacans between the York and James rivers, above the falls.

Powhatan lived sometimes at a village of his name, where Richmond now stands, and sometimes at Werowocomoco, on the York River. He had in each of his hereditary villages a house built like a long arbour for his especial reception. When Powhatan visited one of these villages a feast was already spread in the long house or arbour. He had a hunting town in the wilderness called Orapax. A mile from this place, deep in the woods, he had another arbour-like house, where he kept furs, copper, pearls, and beads, treasures which he was saving against his burial.

Powhatan had twenty sons and eleven daughters living. We know nothing of his sons except Nanteguas, "the most manliest, comliest, boldest spirit" ever seen in "a savage." Pocahontas was Powhatan's favourite daughter. She was born in 1594 or 1595. Of her mother nothing is known. Powhatan had many wives; when he tired of them he would present them to those of his subjects whom he considered the most deserving.

Indians are frequently known by several names. It is a disappointment to learn that the name which the romantic story of this Indian princess has made so famous was not her real name. She was called in childhood Metoax, or Metoake. Concealing this from the English, because of a superstitious notion that if these pale-faced strangers knew her true name they could do her some harm, the Indians gave her name as Pocahontas.

Powhatan's authority, like that of all Indian chiefs, was held in check by custom. "The lawes whereby he ruleth," says Captain Smith, "is custome. Yet when he listeth, his will is a law, and must be obeyed: not only as a king, but as halfe a god they esteeme him."

Each village and tribe had its respective chief, or "werowance," as he was called among the Powhatan Indians. The affairs of the tribe were settled in a council of the chiefs and warriors of the several villages.

Powhatan was the great werowance over all, "unto whom," says Captain Smith, "they pay tribute of skinnes, beads, copper, pearle, deere, turkies, wild beasts, and corne. What he commandeth they dare not disobey in the least thing. It is strange to see with what care and adoration all these people do obey this Powhatan. For at his feete they present whatsoever he commandeth, and at the least frown of his brow, their greatest spirits will tremble! and no marvell, for he is very terrible and tyrannous in punishing such as offend him."

It was a barbarous life in which the little Pocahontas was bred. Her people always washed their young babies in the river on the coldest mornings to harden them. She was accustomed to see her old father sitting at the door of his cabin regarding with grim pleasure a string of his enemy's scalps, suspended from tree to tree, and waving in the breeze. Men in England in her time idealised her into a princess and fine lady. In our time historians have been surprised and indignant at finding that she was not a heroine of romance, but simply an Indian maiden. Such as her life made her she was—in her manners an untrained savage. But she was also the steadfast friend and helper of the feeble colony, and that is why her life is heroic and full of interest.

Powhatan, sensible of the pomp and dignity proper to his position as a great warrior, particularly desired to impress the English who were settling at Jamestown. A member of the colony,

Captain Smith had been prisoner for several weeks and was detained until preparations had been made to receive him in state.

When Powhatan and his train had had time to deck themselves in all "their greatest braveries," Captain Smith was admitted to the chief's presence. He was seated upon a sort of divan resembling a bedstead. Before him was a fire, and on either hand sat two young women about eighteen years of age. Powhatan, "well beaten with many cold and stormy winters," wore strings of pearls around his neck, and was covered with a great robe of raccoon skins decorated with the tails. Around the council house was ranged a double row of warriors. Behind these were as many women. The heads and shoulders of the Indians were painted red, many had their hair decorated with white down, and all wore some savage ornament.

On the appearance of the prisoner a great shout arose from these primitive courtiers. An Indian woman was appointed to bring water for the prisoner to wash his hands in. Another woman brought him feathers to dry them and Captain Smith was then feasted in the "best barbarous manner," and a council was held to decide his fate. This debate lasted a long time, but the conclusion could hardly have been favourable to Captain Smith, since Powhatan was jealous of the white colony already encroaching upon his seclusion at Werowocomoco.

During this solemn debate Captain Smith must have felt anything but comfortable. He did not know his doom until two stones were brought in and placed before Powhatan. Then as many as could lay hands on him dragged him to the feet of the chief and laid his head upon the stones. The executioners raised their clubs to beat out his brains. Such a scene was not uncommon in this forest court. From childhood these savage men and women were accustomed to exult in the most barbarous tortures and executions. It is then the more wonderful that the heart of a little Indian maiden should have been touched with pity for the doomed white man. Pocahontas, a child of ten or twelve, and "the king's dearest daughter," pleaded for the life of the captive. But "no entreaty could prevail" with the stern Powhatan.

The warriors were ready to strike the blow, when the child flew to the side of Captain Smith, took "his head in her arms and laid her own upon his to save him from death, whereat," says the quaint narrative "the Emperor [Powhatan] was contented he should live to make him hatchets and her beads and copper," thinking he was accustomed to follow all occupations. "For," says the story, "the king himself will make his own robes, shoes, bows, arrows, and pots," while he would "plant, hunt, or do any thing so well as the rest."

Powhatan did not long detain Captain Smith for such trivial uses as making trinkets for Pocahontas. It had become the desire of his heart to possess the powerful weapons and tools of the English. He saw that a friend in Jamestown would be a good thing, and he perhaps hoped from friendly commerce with the colony to acquire ascendancy over other Indian tribes.

He took occasion to express his wishes to Captain Smith in a curious manner.

Two days after his rescue from death he had the captive taken to one of his arbour-like buildings in the woods and left alone upon a mat by the fire. The house was curtained off in the centre with a mat. Soon a most doleful noise came from behind the mat, and Powhatan, disguised in "the most fearfullest manner," and looking "more like a devil than a man," entered, with some two hundred Indians, painted black. The outcome of this impressive ceremony was that Powhatan told Captain Smith that they were now friends, and that he would presently send him home, and that when he arrived at Jamestown he must send him two great guns and a grindstone. In return he said he would give him the country of Capahowosick, and would always consider him his son.

Captain Smith was accordingly sent to Jamestown with twelve guides. The Indians delayed on their journey, though the distance was short. They camped in the woods one night, and feasted sumptuously; but Captain Smith was in constant fear of his life still, "expecting every hour to be put to one death or another." He was, however, led in safety to the fort. Here he treated his savage guides with great hospitality, and showed Rawhunt, a trusty servant of Powhatan, two demi-culverins (long cannons carrying a nine-pound shot) and a mill-stone to carry to his chief. The Indians however, "found them somewhat too heavy." For their benefit, Captain Smith had the guns loaded with stones, and discharged among the boughs of trees covered with icicles. The crashing fall of the ice-laden limbs so frightened the Indians that they fled, "half dead with fear," and it was some time before they could be induced to return. Presents of various toys were given them for Powhatan and his family, and they went away satisfied.

The winter of 1607-08 was remarkably cold, both in Europe and America. In the midst of its severity an accident resulted in a fire which destroyed many of the reed-thatched cottages, the palisades, and much of the provisions of the colonists at Jamestown.

Powhatan still looked with covetous eyes upon the glittering swords, the ponderous muskets, and the serviceable pistols of the English. So long as the white man used supernatural bullets and sharp-edged swords and the red man possessed only tomahawks of stone and stone-pointed arrows and javelins, so long were the English safe from Indian attacks. It was now the ambition of Powhatan's life to obtain a goodly store of English weapons, instead of the rude wooden swords used by the Indians. Savage-like, he went about his purpose in the most crafty way with the most innocent air. And sent twenty turkeys "to express his love," with the request that Captain Smith would return the compliment with a present of twenty swords. But Smith refused, knowing it would cut the throat of the colony to put such weapons into the hands of the crafty chief.

Powhatan was not to be thus outdone. If he could not procure the swords in one way he would in another. "He caused his people with twenty devices to obtain" as many swords. The Indians became "insolent." They surprised the colonists at their work. They would lie in ambuscade at the very gates of Jamestown and procure the weapons of stragglers by force. The council in England had deemed it the only wise policy to keep peace with the savages at all hazards, and a wise policy it was if it were not carried too far. The orders from this body had been very strict; the colonists were in no way to offend the Indians.

Thus a "charitable humour prevailed" until Captain Smith was the man they "meddled" with. This fiery soldier did not wait for deliberation. He hunted the miscreants, and those whom he captured he "terrified" with whipping and imprisonment. In return, the Indians captured two straggling Englishmen, and came in force to the very gates of Jamestown, demanding seven Indians, whom, "for their villainies," Smith had detained. The irrepressible Captain immediately headed a sally in which he forced the Indians to surrender the Englishmen unconditionally. He then examined his prisoners, but they were faithful to their chief, and he could get nothing from them. He made six of them believe, by "several volleys of shot," that he had caused one of their number to be killed. They immediately confessed, in separate examinations, to a plot on the part of Powhatan to procure the weapons, and then to cut the throats of the colonists. Captain Smith still detained the Indians, resolving to give them a wholesome fright.

Pocahontas presently came to Jamestown, accompanied by Indian messengers. Her father had sent them with presents, and a message excusing "the injuries done by some rash, untoward captains, his subjects, desiring their liberties for this time with the assurance of his love forever."

When Captain Smith had punished his seven prisoners as he thought fit, he "used them well" for a few days, and delivered them to Pocahontas, pretending that he saved their lives only for the sake of the little Indian girl.

One cannot refrain from admiring in the brave colonists and their captain the fortitude and persistence that they showed, and the wonderful tact with which they managed the natives. Many had died, some had recovered, and others were still sick.

Captain Smith had been installed as president. He governed the colony wisely. His measures were doubtless severe, but severity was necessary among these men totally unqualified for a frontier life, with an unwise management in England, and endless discontent and jealousy at Jamestown. Men shut up together in hard circumstances are sure to fall out.

Captain Smith went energetically to work to better the condition of the colony. Jamestown was once more the scene of busy activity. Church and storehouse were repaired, new houses built for more supplies, and the fort altered in form. The soldiers were drilled every day upon a plain called Smithfield. Here crowds of Indians would gather to watch with wonder the Englishmen shoot at a mark.

Captain Smith, to quiet all fears, and to show his willingness to assist in the business on hand, as well as to hasten an affair which would consume so much valuable time, undertook with four companions a journey to Werowocomoco, to ask Powhatan to come to Jamestown.

It was now the season to trade for corn with the Indians.

*   *   *   *   *

When the Englishmen reached the home of Powhatan they found that he was some thirty miles away. They were received by the steadfast friend of all white men, Pocahontas. She sent messengers for her father, and undertook to entertain her friends while they waited.

The Englishmen were left in an open space, seated on a mat by the fire. Suddenly they heard a "hideous noise" in the woods. Supposing that Powhatan and his warriors were upon them, they sprang to their feet, grasped their arms and seized two or three old Indians who were near them. Pocahontas came to them, however, with her apology, saying that they might kill her "if any hurt were intended." Those who stood near, men, women and children, assured the white men that all was right. Presently thirty young women came rushing out of the woods. Their only covering was a cincture or apron of green leaves; they were gaily painted, some one colour and some another. Every girl wore a pair of deer's horns on her head, while from her girdle and upon one arm hung an otter's skin. The leader wore a quiver of arrows, and carried a bow and arrow in her hands. The others followed with swords, clubs and pot-sticks.

"These fiends, with most hellish shouts and cries," says the ungallant narrator, "cast themselves in a ring about the fire, singing and dancing with most excellent ill variety." This masquerade lasted about half an hour, when the Indian girls disappeared as they had come.

They again reappeared in their ordinary costume. Pocahontas invited Captain Smith to a dinner which had been spread for him with "all the savage dainties" which they could procure. They tormented the captain by pressing around him saying, "Love you not me? Love you not me?" While he feasted they danced, and ended by conducting him to his lodging with fire-brands for torches.

✻   ✻   ✻   ✻   ✻

Powhatan arrived the next day. Cold weather had come and famine began to stare the colonists in the face. The president set out for the country of the Nansemond Indians. These people refused not only to provide the four hundred bushels of corn which they had promised in their treaty with the colonists on their previous visit, but they refused to trade at all. Their excuse was that they had used up the most that they had, and that they were under commands from Powhatan neither to trade with the English nor to allow them to enter their river. The English had recourse to force, and the Indians fled at the first volley of musketry without shooting a single arrow. The first cabin the white men discovered they set on fire. The Indians immediately desired peace, and promised the English half that they had. Before night all the boats were loaded with corn, and the English sailed some four miles down the river. Here they camped out for the night in the open woods on frozen ground covered with snow.

The manner in which these adventurers of nearly three hundred years ago made themselves comfortable is interesting. They would dig away the snow and build a great fire, which would serve to dry and warm the ground. They would then scrape away the fire, spread a mat on the place where it had been, and here they would sleep with another mat hung up as a shield against the wind. In the night, as the wind shifted, they would change their hanging mat, and when the ground grew cold they would again remove their fire and take its place. Their story says that many "a cold winter night" did the adventurers sleep thus; and yet those who went on these expeditions "were always in health, lusty and fat."

Finding that the old Indian chief had determined to starve the colony out of existence by a refusal to trade with the white men, Captain Smith, appreciating the desperate extremity, resolved to take, as usual, the boldest plan out of the difficulty. He meditated a plan for surprising and entrapping Powhatan into his power. Smith saw no other chance to procure food, and starving men do not stop to debate whether a course is right or wrong.

About this time Powhatan sent a message to Smith inviting him to visit him, and saying that if he would but build him a house, give him a grindstone, fifty swords, some firearms, a hen and rooster, and much beads and copper, he would fill the ship with corn. Captain Smith made haste to accept this offer. He sent some of the Dutchmen and some Englishmen ahead to begin the building of Powhatan's house.

On the twelfth of January the English neared Werowocomoco. The ice extended nearly half a mile from shore in the York River. Captain Smith pushed as near the shore as he could in the barge, by breaking the ice. Impatient of remaining in an open boat in the freezing cold, he jumped into the half-frozen marsh, and waded ashore. His example was followed by eighteen of his men.

The English quartered at the first cabins they reached, and announced their arrival in a message to Powhatan, requesting provision. The chief sent them plenty of bread, venison and turkeys, and feasted them according to his custom. The following day, however, he desired to know when they "would be gone," pretending that he had not sent for the English. He made the astonishing statement that he himself had no corn, and his people had much less; but that he would furnish them forty baskets of this grain for as many swords. Captain Smith quickly confronted him with the men who had brought Powhatan's message to Jamestown, and asked the chief "how it chanced he became so forgetful." Powhatan answered with "a merry laughter," and invited the English to show their commodities. But the crafty chief was not suited with anything, unless it were guns or swords.

"Powhatan," said Captain Smith, "believing your promises to supply my wants, I neglected all to satisfy your desire, and to testify my love I sent you my men for your building, neglecting mine own. As for swords and guns, I told you long ago I had none to spare, and you must know those I have can keep me from want. Yet steal or wrong you I will not, nor dissolve that friendship we have mutually promised, except you constrain me by your bad usage."

Powhatan listened attentively to this speech, and promised that he would spare them what he could, which he would deliver to them in two days.

"Yet, Captain Smith," said the chief, "I have some doubt of your coming hither that makes me not so kindly seek to relieve you as I would, for many do inform me your coming hither is not for trade, but to invade my people and possess my country, who dare not bring you corn, seeing you thus armed with your men. To free us of this fear, leave aboard your weapons, for here they are needless, we being all friends."

But Captain Smith was not to be cajoled into a council without weapons. That night was spent at Werowocomoco, and the following day the building of Powhatan's house went forward.

Meanwhile the English managed "to wrangle" some ten bushels of corn out of the chief for a copper kettle.

The chief was dissatisfied that he could not have his way.

"Captain Smith," said Powhatan with a sigh, "I never used any werowance so kindly as yourself, yet from you I receive the least kindness of any. Another captain gave me swords, copper, clothes, a bed, towels or what I desired, ever taking what I offered him, and would send away his guns when I entreated him; none doth deny to lie at my feet or refuse to do what I desire but only you, of whom I can have nothing but what you regard not, and yet you will have whatsoever you demand. You call me father, but I see you will do what you list, and we must seek to content you. But if you intend so friendly as you say, send hence your arms, that I may believe you."

The wily old chief was right. Captain Smith was determined to have his own way. He saw that nothing could be gained thus. Powhatan was watching with lynx eyes for a chance to get the white men into his power while he delivered eloquent and persuasive speeches. Captain Smith asked the savages to break the ice for him that his boat might reach the shore, to take him and the corn. He intended, when the boat came, to land more men and surprise the chief. Meanwhile, to entertain Powhatan and keep him from suspecting anything, he made the following reply to his last speech:

"Powhatan, you must know as I have but one God I honour but one king, and I live not here as your subject, but as your friend, to pleasure you with what I can. By the gifts you bestow on me you gain more than by trade, yet would you visit me as I do you, you should know it is not our custom to sell our courtesies. To content you, to-morrow I will leave my arms and trust to your promise. I call you father indeed, and as a father you shall see I will love you; but the small care you have for such a child caused my men to persuade me to look to myself."

But Powhatan was not to be fooled. His mind was on the fast disappearing ice. He managed to disengage himself from the captain's conversation, and secretly fled with his women, children and luggage. To avoid any suspicion, two or three women were left to engage Captain Smith in talk while warriors beset the house where they were. When Captain Smith discovered what they were doing, he and John Russell went about making their way out with the help of their pistols, swords and Indian shields. At the first shot the savages tumbled "one over another" and quickly fled in every direction, and the two men reached their companions in safety.

✳   ✳   ✳   ✳   ✳

Powhatan saw that his stratagem had failed. He immediately tried to remove the unfavourable impression which this event and the sudden appearance of so many warriors might make on the minds of the English. He sent an "ancient orator" to Captain Smith with presents of a great bracelet and chain of pearls.

"Captain Smith," said the Indian, "our werowance has fled, fearing your guns, and knowing when the ice was broken there would come more men; he sent these numbers but to guard his corn from stealing. Now since the ice is open, he would have you send away your corn, and if you would have his company, send away also your guns, which so affrighteth his people that they dare not come to you as he promised they should."

The Indians provided baskets that the English might carry their corn to the boat. They were officious in tendering their services to guard the colonists' arms while they were thus occupied, lest any one should steal them. There were crowds of those grim, sturdy savages about; but the sight of the white men cocking their matchlock guns rendered them exceedingly meek. They were easily persuaded by this sight to leave their bows and arrows in charge of the Englishmen, while they themselves carried the corn down to the boats on their own backs. This they did with wonderful dispatch.

Ebb tide left the boat stuck in the marsh, and the adventurers were obliged to remain at Werowocomoco until high water. They returned to the cabins where they were at first quartered. The savages entertained them until night with "merry sports," and then left them. Powhatan was gathering his forces and planning the certain destruction of his visitors. The English were alone in the Indian cabins. Suddenly Pocahontas, Powhatan's "dearest jewel and daughter," as she is styled in the quaint narrative, appeared before Captain Smith. She had come this dark night through the "irksome woods" alone from her father's cabin.

"Captain Smith," said she, "great cheer will be sent you by and by; but Powhatan and all the power he can make will after come and kill you all, if they that bring you the cheer do not kill you with your own weapons when you are at supper. Therefore, if you would live, I wish you presently to be gone."

Captain Smith wished to give Pocahontas presents of those trifles dear to the heart of an Indian, and such as Pocahontas most delighted in.

"I dare not," said the girl, with tears running down her cheeks, "be seen to have any, for if Powhatan should know it, I am but dead."

She then ran away into the woods as she had come. Within less than an hour, eight or ten savages came, bringing great platters of venison and other food. They begged the Englishmen to put out the matches of their guns, for the "smoke made them sick," and to sit down to eat. But the Captain was vigilant. He made the Indians first taste of every dish, and he then sent them back to Powhatan, asking him, "to make haste," for he was awaiting his arrival. Soon after more messengers came, "to see what news," and they were followed in a short time by still more. Thus the night was spent by both parties with the utmost vigilance, though to all appearances they were on very friendly terms. When high water came the English prepared to depart. At Powhatan's request they left a man named Edward Brynton to hunt for him, while the Dutchmen remained to finish his house.

On an eminence near where Werowocomoco must have been, still stands a stone chimney which is known to this day as "Powhatan's Chimney," and according to tradition is the chimney of the house which the colonists erected for this chief.

For several years Powhatan continued to be hostile to the colonists. In one way and another he possessed himself of many English arms, and detained a number of Englishmen as prisoners. Some time after this Pocahontas happened to be among the Potomacs on the river of that name. One account says that she had gone thither, feasting among her friends, but another writer of that time says that she had been sent to the Potomacs to trade with them. Perhaps also Powhatan distrusted her friendship for the whites. Whatever may have been the cause, Pocahontas was certainly making a stay on the Potomac River.

The English Captain Argall had gone to trade with the Indians on the Potomac. Some friendly Indians informed him that Pocahontas was in the region. A plan for bringing Powhatan to terms immediately suggested itself to the unscrupulous captain. He sent for one of the Indian chiefs, and told him that if he did not give Pocahontas into his hands they would no longer be "brothers nor friends." The Potomac Indians were at first unwilling to do this, fearing that it might involve them in a war with Powhatan. Captain Argall assured them that he would take their part in such a war, and they consented to his plan.

The following story is told of the manner in which Pocahontas was betrayed. The Indian girl manifested no desire to go aboard Captain Argall's vessels, having many a time been on English vessels, in her friendly relations with the whites. Captain Argall offered an old Indian named Japazaws the irresistible bribe of a copper kettle if he would betray Pocahontas into his power. Japazaws undertook to do this with the assistance of his wife. This wife became immediately possessed with an intense desire to visit the English ship, which she said had been there three or four times and she had never been aboard it. She begged her husband to allow her to go aboard, but Japazaws sternly refused, saying she could not go unless she had some woman to accompany her. He at last threatened to beat her for her persistence.

The tender heart of Pocahontas was moved with pity; she offered to accompany the woman on board the English vessel. Japazaws and his wife with the chief's daughter were taken on to the ship, where they were well entertained and invited to supper. The old man and his wife were so well pleased with their success that during the whole meal they kept treading on Captain Argall's toes. After supper the captain sent Pocahontas to the gun-room while he pretended to have a private conversation with Japazaws. He presently recalled her, and told her that she must remain with him, and that she should not again see Powhatan until she had served to bring about a peace between her father and the English. Immediately Japazaws and his wife set up "a howl and cry," and Pocahontas began to be "exceedingly pensive and discontented." The old people were rowed to shore, happy in the possession of their copper kettle and some trinkets.

Captain Argall sent an Indian messenger to Powhatan, informing him that "his delight and darling, his daughter Pocahontas," was a prisoner, and informing him that "if he would send home the Englishmen whom he had detained in slavery, with such arms and tools as the Indians had gotten and stolen, and also a great quantity of corn, that then he should have his daughter restored, otherwise not."

Powhatan was "very much grieved," having a strong affection both for his daughter and for the English weapons which he possessed. It was a hard alternative. He sent, however, a message desiring the English to use Pocahontas well, and promising to perform the conditions for her rescue.

＊　　＊　　＊　　＊　　＊

It was a long time before anything more was heard from Powhatan. After three months he sent to the governor by way of ransom seven Englishmen, overjoyed to be free from slavery and the constant fear of cruel death, three muskets, a broadaxe, a whip-saw, and a canoe full of corn. These were accompanied by a message to the effect that he would satisfy injuries, give the English a large quantity of corn, and be forever their friend when his daughter was delivered up. The English received these things "in part payment," and returned such an answer as this to Powhatan:

"Your daughter shall be well used, but we cannot believe the rest of our arms are either lost or stolen from you, and therefore, till you send them we will keep your daughter."

The wily old chief was much grieved at this message, and it was again a long time before anything was heard from him. At last Sir Thomas Dale, then the governor of the colony, taking with him Pocahontas and one hundred and fifty men, embarked in the colony's vessels for a visit to Powhatan. The party sailed up the York River. Powhatan was not to be seen. The English told the Indians that they had come to deliver up the daughter of Powhatan and to receive the promised return of men and arms. These overtures were received with scornful threats and open hostility. Skirmishing ensued, in which some of the Indian houses were burned and property spoiled.

The Indians asked why this had been done. The English answered by asking why they had shot at them. The Indians excused themselves, laying the blame on some straggling savages. They protested they intended no harm, but were the white man's friends. The English rejoined that they did not come to hurt them, but came as friends.

A peace was patched up and messengers were sent to Powhatan. The Indians told the English that their imprisoned men "were run off" for fear the English would hang them, but that Powhatan's men "were run after to bring them back." They promised to return them with the stolen swords and muskets on the following day. The English perceived that this story was told only to gain time.

Meantime two brothers of Pocahontas came aboard the ship to visit her. They had heard that she was not well, and were overjoyed to find her in good health and contented. While they were visiting with their sister, Mr. John Rolfe and Mr. Sparks were sent to negotiate with Powhatan. They were received kindly and hospitably entertained, but they were not admitted to the presence of the offended chief. His brother, Opechancanough, saw them and promised to do the best he could with Powhatan, saying that "all might be well." With such slight satisfaction the English were obliged to return to Jamestown, for it was now April and time to sow corn.

Pocahontas had been about a year a prisoner at Jamestown. There can be no doubt that she was treated with the greatest friendliness by the colonists. Her feelings had always been warm for the white strangers. Now that she was an innocent and interesting young prisoner among them, what more natural than that she should be honoured and petted? Pocahontas was now a woman, being about eighteen to nineteen years of age. To judge from her portrait she could not have had the beauty with which tradition has invested her, but she had at least a pleasant and interesting face, and there must have been some charm in her large black eyes and straight black hair.

There was one colonist at least who took a great interest in the young prisoner. Mr. John Rolfe is styled in the different records "an honest gentleman of good behaviour," "an honest and discreet English gentleman," "a gentleman of approved behaviour and honest carriage."

The subject of the conversion of Pocahontas had weighed heavily upon the mind of Mr. Rolfe. He accordingly attempted to convert her to Christianity, and in doing so fell in love with her. Pocahontas became a Christian, and what more natural than that the constant friend of the white men should love an Englishman?

Long before the trip up the York River Mr. Rolfe had loved the Indian maiden. He wrote a long letter to the governor, Sir Thomas Dale, asking his advice. Sir Thomas readily consented to the marriage. Pocahontas, on her part, told her brother of her attachment to Mr. Rolfe. He informed Powhatan, who seemed to have been well pleased with the proposition, for within ten days an old uncle of Pocahontas and two of her brothers arrived at Jamestown. Powhatan had sent them as deputies to witness the marriage of his daughter, and to do his part toward the confirmation of it.

Pocahontas was first baptised. It was deemed necessary to give her a Christian name at her baptism. She was christened Rebecca, and as a king's daughter she was known after this as the Lady Rebecca, and sometimes as the Lady Pocahontas.

In April, 1614, the odd bridal procession moved up the little church with its wide-open windows and its cedar pews. The bridegroom was a young Englishman, the bride an Indian chief's daughter, accompanied by two red-skinned warriors, her brothers. Before the altar with its canoe-like front Pocahontas repeated in imperfect English her marriage vows, and received her wedding ring. The wedding is briefly mentioned by the old recorders only as something bearing upon the welfare of the colony. It was the first union between the people who were to possess the land and the natives. The colonists doubtless regarded it as a most auspicious event, binding as it did the most powerful chief in Virginia to their interests.

From this day friendly intercourse and trade were again established with Powhatan and his people. To the day of his death the old chief never violated the peace which was thus brought about.

In still another way the marriage of Pocahontas benefited the colony. The nearest neighbours of the English were the Chickahominys, a powerful tribe of Indians who were just now free from the yoke of Powhatan, whom they regarded as a tyrant. They had taken advantage of the recent differences between this chief and the colonists to hold themselves exceedingly independent of both. But now that Powhatan and the English were united, the Chickahominys began to fear for their own liberty. They sent a deputation to Sir Thomas Dale desiring peace. Dale visited them, entered their council, and concluded a treaty stipulating that the Chickahominy Indians should call themselves Tassantessus, or Englishmen, as a sign of friendship, and fulfil other conditions.

*　　*　　*　　*　　*

Sir Thomas Dale had been five years in Virginia when in 1616 he settled the affairs of the colony, and embarked for England. He took with him Mr. Rolfe, Pocahontas, Tomocomo, one of Powhatan's chief men, married to his daughter, Matachanna, and other Indians. Tomocomo, who was considered among the Indians "an understanding fellow," had been charged by Powhatan to count the people in England and give him an exact idea of their strength.

The vessel reached Plymouth on the 12th of June, 1616. On leaving the vessel Tomocomo was prepared with a long stick and a knife ready to make a notch for every man he saw. He kept this up till "his arithmetic failed him." We can imagine the excitement that followed these travellers everywhere. They were all wonders, but especially was the "Princess" Pocahontas.

Pocahontas was now mother to a little son, Thomas Rolfe, whom she "loved most dearly." Immediately on her arrival the Virginia Company took measures for the maintenance of her and her child. Persons of great "rank and quality" took much notice of Pocahontas. She did not like the smoke of London, and was removed to Brentford.

Captain Smith was at this time between two voyages and his stay in London was limited. He met Tomocomo, and they renewed old acquaintance.

"Captain Smith," said the Indian, "Powhatan did bid me find you out, to show me your God, and the king and queen and prince you so much had told us of."

"Concerning God," says Smith, in writing of this meeting, "I told him the best I could, the king I heard he had seen, and the rest he should see when he would." Tomocomo, however, denied having seen King James till Smith satisfied him that he had by the circumstances. Tomocomo immediately looked very melancholy and said:

"You gave Powhatan a white dog, which Powhatan fed as himself, but your king gave me nothing, and I am better than your white dog."

Captain Smith, desiring to return the courtesy of Pocahontas, wrote the following letter to Queen Anne immediately upon hearing of the arrival of Pocahontas:

To the most high and virtuous Princess, Queen Anne of Great Britain

Most admired Queen: The love I bear my God, my king, and country hath so oft emboldened me in the worst of extreme dangers, that now honesty doth constrain me to presume thus far beyond myself to present Your Majesty this short discourse. If ingratitude be a deadly poison to all honest virtues, I must be guilty of that crime if I should omit any means to be thankful.

So it is that some ten years ago, being in Virginia, and taken prisoner by the power of Powhatan, their chief king, I received from this great savage exceeding great courtesy, especially from his son Nantequas, the most manliest, comeliest, boldest spirit I ever saw in a savage, and his sister Pocahontas, the king's most dear and well-beloved daughter, being but a child of twelve or thirteen years of age, whose compassionate, pitiful heart, of desperate estate, gave me much cause to respect her. I being the first Christian this proud king and his grim attendants ever saw, and thus enthralled in their barbarous power, I cannot say that I felt the least occasion of want that was in the power of those mortal foes to prevent, notwithstanding all their threats.

After some six weeks fatting among these savage courtiers, at the minute of my execution she hazarded the beating out of her own brains to save mine; and not only that, but so prevailed with her father that I was safely conducted to Jamestown, where I found about eight-and-thirty miserable, poor and sick creatures to keep possession of all those large territories of Virginia. Such was the weakness of this poor commonwealth as, had the savages not fed us, we directly had starved.

And this relief, most gracious queen, was commonly brought us by this lady, Pocahontas. Notwithstanding all these passages when inconstant fortune turned our peace to war, this tender virgin would still not spare to dare to visit us; and by her our jars have oft been appeased and our wants still supplied. Were it the policy of her father thus to employ her, or the ordinance of God thus to make her his instrument, or her extraordinary affection to our nation, I know not. But of this I am sure, when her father, with the utmost of his policy and power sought to surprise me, the dark night could not affright her from coming through the irksome woods, and with watered eyes gave me intelligence, with her best advice to escape his fury; which had he known he had surely slain her. Jamestown, with her wild train, she as freely frequented as her father's habitation; and, during the time of two or three years, she, next, under God, was still the instrument to preserve this colony from death, famine, and utter confusion, which if in those times had once been dissolved, Virginia might have lain as it was at our first arrival to this day.

Since then this business having been turned and varied by many accidents from that I left it at. It is most certain after a long and troublesome war after my departure, betwixt her father and our colony, all which time she was not heard of, about two years after she herself was taken prisoner. Being so detained near two years longer, the colony by that means was relieved, peace concluded, and at last, rejecting her barbarous condition, she was married to an English gentleman, with whom at present she is in England; the first Christian ever of that nation, the first Virginian ever spoke English: a matter surely, if my meaning be truly considered and well understood, worthy a prince's understanding.

Thus, most gracious lady, I have related to Your Majesty what at your best leisure our approved histories will account you at large, and done in the time of Your Majesty's life. And, however, this might be presented to you from a more worthy pen, it cannot come from a more honest heart, as yet I never begged anything of the State or any; and it is my want of ability and her exceeding desert, your birth, means and authority, her birth, virtue, want and simplicity, doth make me thus bold humbly to beseech your majesty to take this knowledge of her, though it be from one so unworthy to be the reporter as myself, her husband's estate not being able to make her fit to attend your majesty. The most and least I can do is to tell you this, because none hath so oft tried it as myself; and the rather being of so great a spirit, however her stature. If she should not be well received, seeing this kingdom may rightly have a kingdom by her means, her present love to us and Christianity might turn to such scorn and fury as to divert all this good to the worst of evil; where, finding so great a queen should do her some honour more than she can imagine, for being so kind to your servants and subjects, would so ravish her with content, as endear her dearest blood to effect that Your Majesty and all the king's honest subjects most earnestly desire. And so I humbly kiss your gracious hands.

Captain Smith went to Brentford with several others to see Pocahontas. She saluted him modestly, and without a word turned round and "obscured her face as not seeming well contented." Smith, with her husband and the other gentlemen, left her "in that humour" for several hours. The captain was disappointed, and repented having written the queen that she could speak English. But when the gentlemen returned Pocahontas began to talk, and said that she remembered Captain Smith well, "and the courtesies she had done."

"You did promise Powhatan," said Pocahontas, "what was yours should be his, and he the like to you. You called him father, being in his land a stranger, and by the same reason so must I do to you."

Captain Smith tried to excuse himself from this honour. He "durst not allow that title because she was a king's daughter."

"Were you not afraid," said Pocahontas, with a look of determination, "were you not afraid to come into my father's country, and caused fear in him and all his people but me, and fear you here I should call you father? I tell you then I will, and you shall call me child, and so I will be forever and ever your countryman. They did tell us always you were dead, and I knew no other until I came to Plymouth; yet Powhatan did command Tomocomo to seek you and know the truth, because your countrymen will lie much."

Pocahontas had really felt a warm affection for Smith as a friend of her childhood.

Pocahontas, it is said, had been so well instructed that she "was become very formal and civil after our English manner." During his brief stay in London Captain Smith made frequent visits to Pocahontas, accompanied by courtiers and other friends who wished to see the Indian lady. The gentlemen, said Smith, "generally concluded they did not think God had a great hand in her conversion," and said that they had seen "many English ladies worse favoured, proportioned, and behavioured."

While Pocahontas was in England her portrait was drawn and engraved. She is represented in the fashionable costume of the day. Beneath the picture were these words:

Matoaks als Rebecka, daughter to the mighty Prince Powhatan, Emperor of Attanough-kornouck als Virginia, converted and baptised in the Christian faith, and wife to the worshipful Mr. John Rolfe. Aged 21. Anno Domini 1616.

Pocahontas was destined never to return to America. She died at Gravesend on the eve of her departure for America, being about twenty-two years of age. The few words devoted in Smith's History to her death are quite characteristic of the times:

It pleased God at Gravesend to take this young lady to His mercy, where she made not more sorrow for her unexpected death than joy to the beholders to hear and see her make so religious and godly an end.

In the parish register at Gravesend is the following blundering entry, which could hardly have referred to any other than Pocahontas:

**1616, May 2j, Rebecca Wrothe
wyff of Thomas Wroth gent.
a Virginian lady borne, here was buried
in ye channcell.**

The child of Pocahontas was left in England in the care of Sir Lewis Stewkley, and afterwards transferred to the care of his uncle, Mr. Henry Rolfe, a London merchant. He was educated in England and afterwards returned to America. From him descended some of the most respectable families in Virginia. There is on record a petition signed by Pocahontas's son, Thomas Rolfe, and addressed to the authorities of the colony in 1641, praying to be allowed to go to the Indian country to visit his mother's sister, known among the white people as Cleopatra.

IX

FLORA MACDONALD

In the year 1745 Charles Edward, commonly called the "Young Pretender" to the throne of England and Scotland, landed in Scotland and raised the standard of revolt. He was followed by many of the Highland clans and also by certain of the Lowland. At the head of five thousand men he advanced into England, but he was forced to retreat, and after the battle of Culloden became a fugitive from the pursuing English.

At last he found himself in the Islands of the Hebrides off the northwest coast of Scotland where he hoped to escape the vessels of war in search of him, and soldiers close upon his tracks, and to find a ship upon which he might sail to France. When, about the middle of May, 1846, he reached the Island of South Uist, he and the two friends who clung to him, found themselves in a most miserable condition. They had lived for several days on dried fish and for still longer subject to inclemencies of weather. In South Uist they sought shelter of a friendly chief.

It required all the hospitable care of the Macdonald of Clanronald, who lived at a place called Ormaclade, to recruit and restore his visitors. A hut, built in a desolate spot among the neighbouring mountains was prepared for the royal adventurer where he awaited, under the friendly care, not only of the island's chief, but of every member of the chieftaincy, means of escape.

When Charles made his appearance at the house of Clanronald, he was in tattered clothing and almost barefoot. Supplied with every necessary, though condemned to the shelter of a miserable shed, and fearing to stir beyond this humble abode, he yet recovered in a degree, his energies, and was strengthened enough to hear that there was no prospect of escape to France. In less time than he had realised, he beheld himself completely hemmed in by sea and land. Several ships of war guarded the coast, and a host of soldiers scoured every probable retreat where the object of their search could be concealed.

In this strait, the islanders, untutored and primitive as they were, vied with each other in giving assistance to their chieftain to preserve his guest's life. Although his retreat was perfectly well known to nearly every inhabitant of the island, neither man, woman nor child ever lisped the secret.

It chanced at this time that Flora, sister to the Macdonald of Milton, who also lived on the island, was upon a visit to her brother, and learned of the peril of the royal fugitive. When visiting her relatives at Ormaclade, this young lady, then in her twenty-fifth year, and possessed of a heroic spirit, became much interested in the visits of one of Charles's friends, O'Neil, to procure necessaries for the prince, and, before long, earnestly expressed her desire to be introduced to him, and to contribute to his escape. It seems that O'Neil had previously met Flora, and, from the estimate he had formed of her capacity, led Charles's mind to dwell greatly upon engaging her assistance to rescue him from danger.

The stepfather of Miss Macdonald was, at that time, employed as commander of the very body of soldiers engaged in the pursuit. He was obliged to act in obedience to the chief of his clan, the laird of Sleat, which is the southern part of the island of Skye; but he secretly endeavoured to assist the fugitive, and was only too happy to afford silent consent to any plan which might be originated for his deliverance.

It was a beautiful June evening when Flora's wish to see the Prince was carried out. O'Neil joined her at the house of one of her brother's retainers, leaving his companion concealed, until he should engage Flora to consent to the plan he had in view. He proposed that she should disguise Charles as a female servant; and under pretext of travelling with her maid, conduct him in safety from Uist to the Isle of Skye; whence further measures could be taken to effect his escape.

This was a proposition that Flora's delicacy, as well as innate prudence, shrank from entertaining. She hesitated, avowing her distrust in the wildness of the scheme, and her fear of compromising her friends, Sir Alexander and Lady Margaret

Macdonald, by taking the fugitive into their neighbourhood. O'Neil, however, with Irish tact, so worked upon the young lady's feelings, by leading forth his hapless Prince just at the right moment, that poor Flora's resolutions melted away before the sight of a figure so attenuated, and a countenance so filled by grief and despair, as those now presented to her gaze. She consented, after a brief interval.

When Flora first saw Charles all the brilliancy and promise of his first arrival had passed away, together with the charm of attractive exterior. Weeks of anxiety had taken the colour from his cheek and fire from his eye. Lack of food had made him emaciated. He was no longer the bold aspirant for the throne of the Stuarts. He was the defeated, hunted scion of the ex-royal family, with a price upon his head.

Upon leaving the Prince, Miss Macdonald and her servant were seized by a band of militia; but difficulty was happily set aside by our heroine's discovery that the band was commanded by her stepfather. With little trouble she engaged his assistance, and obtained from him a pass for herself and her man-servant, Neil Mackechan, back to the Island of Skye, where her mother lived. Mention was also made in the passport, of a third person, an Irish domestic, named "Betty Burke," who was especially recommended by Captain Macdonald to his wife, as an "excellent spinner of flax, and a faithful servant." After getting this document, Flora's next care was to secure a boat, with a crew of six men, a supply of provisions, and last, but most important of all, the disguise intended to transform the elegant Prince Charles into a rough Irish maid-of-all-work, and which consisted of a printed linen gown, a white apron and head gear.

The morning of the 27th of June was chosen for their departure, and, accompanied by Lady Clanronald, Miss Macdonald set out towards the seashore. They found the Prince roasting the liver of a sheep for his dinner, a sight which brought the reverses of fortune forcibly to their minds, and moved one of his gentle visitors to tears. That night an alarm, which drew the ladies back to the house, prevented the boat from starting; but the next evening, all being in readiness, the Prince assumed his linen gown and apron and, exchanging his sword for a good-sized walking-stick, embarked with his fair ally, her servant Mackechan, and six boatmen, for Skye.

It was not one of pleasure, this voyage, to a young and delicate woman, considering the number of vessels lying all around, whose shots it would probably be difficult to avoid if suspicion were excited; the distance to be covered, thirty or forty miles, and the time, night. Soon rain began to fall; the skies and sea faded into one leaden expanse; the boatmen, wet and sulky, relapsed into perfect silence. The voice of the young Prince alone broke the stillness; and he, with a mixture of boyish vivacity and manly tact, told story after story, and sang snatches of song until he succeeded in dispelling the cloud of anxiety which oppressed his companion, less fearful for her own than for his safety. At length, overpowered by fatigue, Flora slept. Charles continued a long while singing, in the hope of lulling her to repose; and when, some time after, she awoke, she found him watching her with the greatest solicitude, endeavouring to screen her from the spray, and to protect her from contact with the sails and cordage.

It must have been an unspeakable relief to the occupants of that little boat when the first dim lines of light in the distant horizon announced the approach of morning. When clear enough to distinguish objects, they discovered that they were alone upon the ocean—no land in sight; but this gave little anxiety to the sailors, and after a short interval, during which the wind favoured their passage, the rocky coast of the mountainous Island of Skye appeared. As they were passing a headland called Vaternish, a party of the Macleod militia, espied them, and fired several shots. Happily, however, the tide was out, and before a boat would be got into deep water, pursuit was hopeless.

"Don't mind the villains, but pull for your lives," cried the Prince, and the boatmen, animated by his address and courage, replied cheerily that they would soon distance their assailants; adding, that if they cared at all, it was only for him.

"Oh, there's no fear for me!" was the response, while the Prince busied himself in taking care of Flora, whom he had persuaded to take shelter in the bottom of the boat, a retreat which, to satisfy her fears, he himself adopted shortly after.

A few miles further, the boat was put into a creek, for the purpose of affording a little rest to the rowers, by this time greatly fatigued. They were soon, however, obliged to put off again, in consequence of being watched from the shore and, proceeding about twelve miles from Vaternish, they reached in safety, Mugstat, the residence of Sir Alexander Macdonald, formerly a staunch Jacobite, or follower of the Stuarts, though now in actual attendance upon the Duke of Cumberland at Fort Augustus.

When the boat containing the fugitive Prince had landed, Flora, attended by Mackechan, proceeded to the house, leaving Charles, in his female dress, sitting on her trunk on the beach. On arriving at the dwelling, she desired a servant to inform Lady Margaret that she had called on her way home from Uist. She was immediately introduced to the family apartment, where she found, besides Mrs. Macdonald of Kirkibost, a Lieutenant Macleod, the commander of militia stationed near, three or four members of which were also in the house. There was also present, Mr. Alexander Macdonald of Kingsburgh, an elderly gentleman of the neighbourhood, who acted as factor to Sir Alexander, and who was, she knew, a sound Jacobite.

Flora entered easily into conversation with the officer, who asked her a number of questions; where she had come from, where she was going, and so forth; all of which she answered without manifesting the least trace of confusion which might have been expected from a young lady under such circumstances. The same man had been in the custom of examining every boat which landed from Long Island; that, for instance, in which Mrs. Macdonald of Kirkibost arrived had been so examined, and we can only account for his allowing that of Miss Flora to pass by the circumstance of his meeting her under the courtesies of the drawing-room of a lady.

Miss Macdonald, with the same self-possession, dined in Lieutenant Macleod's company. Seizing a proper opportunity, she apprised Kingsburgh of the circumstances of the Prince, and he immediately proceeded to another room, and sent for Lady Margaret, that he might break the intelligence to her in private. Notwithstanding the previous warning, she was much alarmed at the idea of the wanderer being so near her house, and immediately sent for a certain Donald Roy Macdonald, to consult as to what should be done. Donald had been wounded in the Prince's army at Culloden, and was as obnoxious to the Government as he could be. He came and joined the lady and her friends in the garden, when it was arranged that Kingsburgh should take the Prince along with him to his own house, some miles distant, and thence pass him through the island to Portree, where Donald Roy should take him up, and provide for his further safety.

No time was lost in dispatching Kingsburgh to communicate these arrangements to the Prince, and to carry him some refreshment. The poor refugee, seeing some one approaching him, started up, and discovering the heavy stick he carried, put himself in an attitude of defiance.

"I am Macdonald of Kingsburgh, come to serve Your Highness," said the old man; and he proceeded to explain how this might be effected.

While these two set off toward Kingsburgh, Miss Macdonald quietly seated with Lady Margaret and the officer before named, endeavoured to secure to them a good start upon their journey. Presently she bade farewell to her hostess, who pretended to be extremely averse to parting with her so soon, and invited her warmly to remain; reminding her that she had promised to pay her a lengthened visit. Flora excused herself, upon the plea that her mother was ill, and needed her presence at home. After dinner, therefore, she departed, leaving young Macleod quite unsuspicious of the real nature of her visit to Mugstat. In after years Flora often rallied this gentleman upon having so completely deceived him.

Mrs. Macdonald of Kirkibost, her servants, and Mackechan, accompanied Flora, whose object was to come up with the pedestrians and, joining them, to proceed all together to Kingsburgh. They soon appeared in sight; but as the servants of her companion were unacquainted with the secret, it was necessary to put them off the scent by passing the travellers, as if unknown to them, at a trot. Charles is represented as being very awkward in his feminine attire: Kingsburgh laughed and said to him.

"Your enemies call you a Pretender; but if you be, I can tell you, you are the worst at the trade I ever saw."

He held up his petticoats in a very undignified manner; and when remonstrated with, improved upon matters by permitting the skirts of his dress to draggle in the water, when a brook again had to be passed. His height was so remarkable, and his strides so immense, that the maid-servant at Flora's side exclaimed to her:

"That must be an Irishwoman, or else a man in woman's clothes; see what steps the creature takes!"

Flora replied that she was doubtless an Irishwoman. Shortly after they parted company, and Flora rejoined the travellers, who had been somewhat annoyed on their side by the inquiries and remarks as to the uncommon height of the pretended Betty Burke. About eleven o'clock at night, the little party arrived in safety at Kingsburgh House, where Mrs. Macdonald received them.

Supper followed, Charles, still in gown and coif, presiding, with his hostess on his left hand, and Flora in the place of honour. After supper the ladies withdrew to discuss past perils and future plans.

"And what," said Lady Kingsburgh, "has been done with the boatmen who brought you to the island?"

"They have been sent back to South Uist," replied the young lady.

"That was an oversight. These men ought to have been detained a short time. I fear that if they meet with Government officers, they may incautiously, or for money, betray our poor wanderer's retreat."

Lady Kingsburgh's surmise, which had even at that early period proved correct, seemed so alarming, that Flora decided upon persuading the Prince to assume, as soon at possible, the dress of his own sex.

The hunted Prince had now been several days without taking off his clothes or enjoying the luxury of a bed. He was only too happy to retire to the one provided for him, and it was now far into the night. He slept until late the following morning, so late, indeed, that Miss Macdonald went into Kingsburgh's room, and urged him to rouse the Prince, and depart with him, lest a party of militia should arrive, and make it impossible to leave the house.

Kingsburgh, however, would by no means consent to disturb the weary outcast he had so generously sheltered. "Let the poor boy sleep after his fatigues," he said. "As for me, I care little if they rake off this old gray head, ten or eleven years sooner than I should die in the course of nature." Saying these words, he turned again to his pillow, and was asleep in a moment.

Toward afternoon the party again set forward, but previously Kingsburgh had provided the Prince with a new pair of shoes, his own being completely worn out. "Look," said this enthusiastic Jacobite, holding up the old ones, "I shall faithfully keep these shoes until you are comfortably settled at St. James. I will then introduce myself by shaking them at you, and thus put you in mind of your night's entertainment and protection under this roof."

"Be as good as your word, my friend," replied the Prince: "whenever that time arrives I shall expect to see you."

It was judged better that, as Flora had come with a female servant, she should take one away with her; so Charles waited to alter his dress until they reached a little wood upon the road to Portree, when he again assumed his male attire, exchanging his petticoat and apron for a tartan coat and waistcoat, a philibeg and short hose, plaid and bonnet. Kingsburgh here bade adieu to the Prince, who, with Mackeckan, was to walk a distance of fourteen miles to Portree, while to avoid suspicion, Flora proceeded thither by another road. Arriving at Portree, Flora detained him no longer than to bid him an earnest, though agitated, farewell. Charles thanked her, in the most animated terms, for all the heroism she had shown in his cause.

"Ah! madam," he said, with emotion, "for all that has happened, I hope we shall meet in St. James's yet."

This was the last time Charles ever saw his generous protectress. They hurried him away to the vessel, while Flora, with a heavy heart, turned her steps toward the house of her mother at Sleat. She had effected all in her power, she had used her best exertions to secure the safety of this, the last unfortunate scion of the old Stuart line, and to Heaven she commended the rest. What vicissitudes the wretched Charles encountered, how he lay, pinched with hunger, and failing in health, in cowsheds, in caves and among bushes and underwood until, three months after, he was able to embark from Lochnanuagh, the very spot where he had landed, and to effect his escape to France, is well known in history. It is probable that, after the part she had taken, after the dangers she had boldly confronted in the endeavour to secure his escape, Flora Macdonald's thoughts were with the fugitive constantly; nor is it to be supposed she ever enjoyed a moment of actual peace of mind until the news of his safe arrival in Brittany reached her.

*   *   *   *   *

Flora Macdonald, after quitting the Prince, proceeded to the house of her mother. Upon her arrival, she checked the confidence which she would otherwise have gladly made, relative to her late employment, fearing to involve others in the danger she herself had incurred. She considered it better, if inquiries were made, that they should be able to declare nothing had been known to them of the Prince's escape. That such inquiries would arise, Flora felt assured; and the result proved how correct was her anticipation. It was only a day or two before she heard that the boatmen, on reaching the island whence they had conveyed the fugitives, had been intimidated into revealing the place where they had left her. A Captain Ferguson, a Government emissary, obtaining the description of "Betty Burke's" appearance, sailed at once for Skye, and finding no "tall female" had been seen there with Miss Macdonald, followed upon the latter's track to Kingsburgh, where he soon discovered from the servants, that the supposed Irish domestic had reappeared, and been accommodated with the best bedchamber in the house. The good old Kingsburgh refusing to give further information, was laid in durance, and threatened with no punishment short of death; while the attendance of Miss Macdonald was commanded without loss of time. In opposition to the advice of her family, Flora wisely determined to obey the summons. On her way she met her stepfather, but was almost immediately after seized by a party of soldiers, and taken to the vessel of the Captain Ferguson named above. Meeting on board General Campbell, she frankly confessed to him the truth of the statement made by her boatmen, and quietly resigned herself prisoner.

It will be remembered that Charles's friend, and ardent admirer—his only follower, indeed, at that time—was Captain O'Neil, the one who had first, from some slight acquaintance with Flora, suggested her aid, and, succeeded in gaining it. On board the ship to which, after twenty-two days Flora was sent, she found this generous and lively young Irishman also a prisoner, and going straight up to him, she tapped him gently with her hand, and said laughingly, "To that black countenance, it seems, I am to owe all my misfortunes." He replied earnestly: "Ah! do not regard as a misfortune what is the brightest honour; only go on as you have begun; neither repent nor be ashamed of what will yet redound to your greatest praise and advantage." This exhortation must have been needless to one of our heroine's temperament.

Owing to the courtesy of those in authority, Flora experienced as well in the ship of Commodore Smith as on board the *Bridgewater*, her next prison, the greatest kindness and indulgence. She was permitted to land and bid her mother farewell, to engage a Scotch attendant, the only girl who could be induced to accompany her, and to secure a portion of her wardrobe, she having been some time deprived of a change of clothing. On arriving at Leith she remained nearly two months in harbour, and was allowed to receive visitors on board, though she was not allowed to leave the ship. The simple-minded country maiden suddenly discovered that she had been transformed into a heroine. The fame of her courage had gone far and wide; everybody was anxious to see her. Many brought presents, and one a Bible and Prayer Book, together with sewing materials, which she joyfully received. It is related that Lady Mary Cochrane paid her a visit, and upon the wind freshening a little, pretended fear of returning to shore, in order that she might, as she said, be able to say she had spent the night with Miss Flora Macdonald.

Arrived in London, Miss Macdonald was placed in the house of a gentleman, where she could scarcely be said to be put under restraint of any disagreeable nature. Here she remained for several months, and upon the passing of the Act of Indemnity, in July of the year, 1747, was set at liberty without the ceremony of a trial. Public opinion was wholly in her favour, and many in power, Frederick, Prince of Wales, father of George III, among the number, made no secret of their approbation of her conduct under the affecting circumstances in which the unhappy Charles Edward had sought her aid.

Shortly after her return home, on November 6, 1750, she was married to young Macdonald, the son of the generous Kingsburgh, and became the mother of five sons, more or less remarkable for the courage and intrepidity ennobling their ancestry on both sides.

When Dr. Johnson went with Boswell to the Hebrides, in the year 1773, he was warmly received by the husband of Flora, then himself possessor of the family mansion in which Charles Edward had been successfully hidden. "Kingsburgh," says Boswell, in his account of the great moralist's tour, "is completely the figure of a gallant Highlander, exhibiting the graceful mien and manly looks which our popular Scotch song has justly attributed to that character. He had jet black hair which was tied behind, and was a large, stately man, with a steady, sensible countenance." Flora herself he describes as a woman of middle stature, soft features, gentle manners, and elegant presence. She was, at this time, fifty-three years old. Lady Kingsburgh spelled her name not "Flora," but "Flory" Macdonald.

The year following this visit of the doctor, the Kingsburghs emigrated to North Carolina, in the hope of effecting a comfortable settlement in America. Their journey was not a fortunate one. The husband of Flora, who appears to have been as brave as ever in the cause he embraced, joining the 84th Royal Highland Emigrant Regiment, was imprisoned by the provincial force; but he was soon set at liberty, and he then joined the North Carolina Highlanders, serving in Canada. Upon the conclusion of the war he returned to Scotland, probably wearied of the incessant harass he had experienced in the New World, and yearning for a sight of his native land. During their homeward voyage the ship was attacked by a French privateer. It would scarcely be in character to suppose our heroine a silent or impassive spectator of the combat. While standing on deck near her husband, and boldly animating the sailors by spirited words and gestures, which even in her old age seemed to have lost nothing of their power, she was thrown down with such violence that the shock broke her arm. In allusion to this accident and the circumstances of it, she is said to have remarked with great coolness, that "she had now suffered a little for both the houses of Stuart and Hanover."

After her return to Skye, Flora never again left it. She lived to be quite an old woman, and her body was followed to the grave by about three thousand persons, friends and retainers, amongst whom many had been recipients of her bounty, and most were capable of estimating the fine qualities of heart and mind which rendered her death a public loss. Besides her sons, all of them officers in the army or navy, Flora Macdonald had two daughters, who were married to gentlemen following the same profession as their brothers. One of the sons, anxious to perpetuate the remembrance of the spot where so heroic and devoted a mortal was buried, sent a marble tablet, commemorative of his mother, to be placed upon her tomb in the churchyard of Kilmuir; but this having been broken by accident, tourists took the opportunity to carry off pieces and, at the present time the grave of Flora Macdonald remains undistinguished within the rude inclosure that holds the dust of so many of the brave Kingsburgh family.

X

MADAME ROLAND

In the year 1754 there was living in an obscure workshop in Paris, an engraver by the name of Gratien Phlippon. He had married a very beautiful woman, whose placid temperament and cheerful content contrasted strikingly with the restlessness of her husband. The comfortable yet humble apartments of the engraver were over the shop where he plied his daily toil. He was much dissatisfied with his lowly condition in life, and that his family, in the enjoyment of frugal competence alone, were debarred from those luxuries which were profusely showered upon others. Bitterly and unceasingly he murmured that his lot had been cast in the ranks of obscurity and of unsparing labour, while others, by a more fortunate, although no better merited destiny, were born to ease and affluence, and honour and luxury. Phlippon was a philosopher. Submission was a virtue he had never learned, and never wished to learn.

Madame Phlippon was just the reverse of her husband. She was a woman in whom faith, and trust, and submission predominated. She surrendered her will, without questioning, to all the teachings of the Church. She was placid, contented and cheerful, and undoubtedly sincere in her piety. In every event of life she recognised the overruling hand of Providence, and feeling that the comparatively humble lot assigned her was in accordance with the will of God, she indulged in no repinings.

Of eight children born to these parents, one only, Jeanne Manon, or Jane Mary, survived the hour of birth. Her father first received her to his arms in 1754, and she became the object of his painful and most passionate adoration. Both parents lived in her and for her. She was their earthly all. Even in her infantile years she gave indication of a most brilliant intellect—and her father repined that she should be doomed to a life of obscurity and toil, while the garden of the Tuileries and the Elysian Fields were thronged with children, neither so beautiful nor so intelligent, who were reveling in boundless wealth, and living in a world of luxury and splendour which, to Phlippon's imagination, seemed more alluring than any idea he could form of heaven.

By nature Jane was endowed with a soul of unusual delicacy. From early childhood, all that is beautiful or sublime in nature, in literature, in character, had charms to rivet her entranced attention. She loved to sit alone at her chamber window in the evening of a summer's day, to gaze upon the gorgeous hues of sunset. Books of poetry and descriptions of heroic character and achievements were her especial delight. "Plutarch's Lives," that book which, more than any other, appears to be the incentive of early genius, was hid beneath her pillow, and read and re-read. Those illustrious heroes of antiquity became the companions of her solitude and of her hourly thoughts. She adored them and loved them as her own most intimate personal friends. Her character became insensibly moulded to their forms, and she was inspired with restless enthusiasm to imitate their deeds. When but twelve years of age her father found her, one day, weeping that she was not born a Roman maiden.

It was, perhaps, the absence of playmates, and the habitual converse with mature minds which, at so early an age, inspired Jane with that insatiate thirst for knowledge which she ever manifested. Books were her only resource in every unoccupied hour. From her walks with her father, and her domestic employments with her mother, she turned to her little library and to her chamber window, and lost herself in the limitless realms of thought.

In a bright summer's afternoon she might be seen sauntering along the boulevards, led by her father's hand, gazing upon that scene of gaiety with which the eye is never wearied. A gilded coach, drawn by the most beautiful horses in the richest trappings, sweeps along the streets—a gorgeous vision. Phlippon takes his little daughter in his arms to show her the sight, and, as she gazes in infantile wonder and delight, the discontented father says:

"Look at that lord and lady, and child, lolling so voluptuously in their coach. They have no right there. Why must I and my child walk on this hot pavement, while they repose on velvet cushions and revel in all luxury? A time will come when the people will awake to the consciousness of their wrongs, and their tyrants will tremble before them."

He continues his walk in moody silence, brooding over his sense of injustice. They return to their home.

Jane wishes that her father kept a carriage, and liveried servants and outriders. She thinks of politics, and of the tyranny of kings and nobles, and of the unjust inequalities of man. She retires to the solitude of her loved chamber window, and reads of Aristides the Just, of Themistocles with his Spartan virtues, of Brutus, and of the mother of the Gracchi. Greece and Rome rise before her in all their ancient renown. She despises the frivolity of Paris and her youthful bosom throbs with the desire of being noble in spirit and of achieving great exploits. Thus, when other children of her age were playing with their dolls, she was dreaming of the prostration of nobles and of the overthrow of thrones.

The education of young ladies, at that time in France, was conducted almost exclusively by nuns in convents. The idea of the silence and solitude of the cloister inspired the highly imaginative girl. Her mother's spirit of religion was exerting a powerful influence over her, and one evening she fell at her mother's feet and, bursting into tears, besought that she might be sent to a convent to prepare to receive her first Christian communion in a suitable frame of mind.

The convent of the sisterhood of the Congregation in Paris was selected for Jane. She subsequently wrote:

While pressing my dear mother in my arms, at the moment of parting with her for the first time in my life, I thought my heart would break; but I was acting in obedience to the voice of God, and I passed the threshold of the cloister, tearfully offering up to him the greatest sacrifice I was capable of making. This was on the 7th of May, 1765, when I was eleven years and two months old. The first night I spent in the convent was a night of agitation. I was no longer under the paternal roof. I was at a distance from that kind mother, who was doubtless thinking of me with affectionate emotion. A dim light diffused through the room in which I had been put to bed with four children of my own age. I stole softly from my couch and drew near the window, the light of the moon enabling me to distinguish the garden, which it overlooked. The deepest silence prevailed around, and I listened to it, if I may use the expression, with a sort of respect. Lofty trees cast their gigantic shadows along the ground, and promised a secure asylum to meditation. I lifted up my eyes to the heavens; they were unclouded and serene. I imagined that I felt the presence of the Deity smiling upon my sacrifice, and already offering me a reward in the hope of a celestial abode. Tears of delight flowed down my cheeks. I repeated my vows with holy ecstasy, and went to bed again to taste the slumber of God's chosen children.

Two years after this she was taken to pass a week at the luxurious abodes of Maria Antoinette. Versailles was in itself a city of palaces and of courtiers, where all that could dazzle the eye in regal pomp and voluptuousness was concentred. Most girls of her age would have been enchanted and bewildered by this display. Jane was permitted to witness, and partially to share, all the pomp of luxuriously spread tables and presentations, and court balls, and illuminations and the gilded equipages of ambassadors and princes, but this maiden, just emerging from the period of childhood and the seclusion of the cloister, undazzled by all this brilliance, looked sadly on the scene. The servility of the courtiers excited her contempt. She contrasted the boundless profusion and extravagance which filled these palaces with the absence of comfort in the dwellings of the over-taxed poor, and pondered deeply the value of that despotism which starved the millions to pander to the dissolute indulgence of the few. Her personal pride was also severely stung by perceiving that her own attractions, mental and physical, were entirely overlooked by the crowds which were bowing before power. Disgusted with the frivolity of the living, she sought solace in companionship with the illustrious dead. She chose the gardens for her resort, and, lingered around the statues which embellished scenes of almost fairy enchantment.

"How do you enjoy your visit, my daughter?" inquired her mother.

"I shall be glad when it is ended," was the characteristic reply, "else, in a few more days, I shall so detest all the persons I see that I shall not know what to do with my hatred."

"Why, what harm have these persons done you, my child?"

"They make me feel injustice and look upon absurdity," replied this philosopher of thirteen.

Soon after this Jane entered her fourteenth year and her mother, conscious of the importance to her child of a knowledge of domestic duties, took her to the market to obtain meat and vegetables, and occasionally placed upon her the responsibility of the family purchases. The unaffected dignity with which the imaginative girl yielded herself to these most prosaic avocations was such, that when she entered the market, the fruit women hastened to serve her. It is quite remarkable that Jane, apparently, never turned with repugnance from these humble avocations of domestic life. It speaks most highly in behalf of the sound judgment of her mother, that she was enabled thus successfully to allure her daughter from her realms of romance to those unattractive practical duties which our daily necessities demand. At one hour this ardent maiden might have been seen in her little chamber absorbed in studies of deepest research. The highest themes which can elevate the mind of man claimed her delighted reveries. The next hour she might be seen in the kitchen, under the guidance of her mother, receiving from her judicious lips lessons upon frugality, and industry, and economy. The white apron was bound around her waist, and her hands, which, but a few moments before, were busy with the circles of the celestial globe, were now occupied in preparing vegetables for dinner. There was thus united in the character of Jane the appreciation of all that is beautiful and sublime in the world of fact and the world of imagination, and also domestic skill and practical common sense. She was thus prepared to fascinate by the graces of a refined and polished mind, and to create for herself, in the midst of all vicissitudes, a region of loveliness in which her spirit could ever dwell; and, at the same time she possessed that sagacity and tact, and those habits of usefulness, which prepared her to meet calmly all the changes of fortune, and over them all to triumph. With that self-appreciation which with her was frankness rather than vanity she subsequently writes:

This mixture of serious studies, agreeable relaxations and domestic cares, was rendered pleasant by my mother's good management, and fitted me for everything. It seemed to forebode the vicissitudes of future life, and enabled me to bear them. In every place I am at home. I can prepare my own dinner with as much address as Philopœmen cut wood; but no one seeing me thus engaged would think it an office in which I ought to be employed.

As years passed on through the friendship of a family of noble rank, Jane was often introduced to the great world. The family became much interested in the fascinating young lady, and her brilliant talents and accomplishments secured her invitations to many social interviews. This slight acquaintance with the nobility of France did not, however, elevate them in her esteem. She found the conversation of the old marquises and antiquated dowagers who frequented the saloon of Madame De Boismorel more insipid and illiterate than that of the tradespeople who visited her father's shop, and upon whom these nobles looked down with contempt. Jane was also disgusted with the many indications she saw, not only of indolence, but of dissipation and utter want of principle. Her good sense enabled her to move among these people as a studious observer of human nature, neither adopting their costume nor imitating their manners. She was very unostentatious and simple in her dress, and never, in the slightest degree, affected the mannerism of mindless and artless fashion.

Madame De Boismorel, at one time eulogising her taste in these respects, remarked:

"You do not love feathers, do you, Miss Phlippon? How very different you are from the giddy-headed girls around us!"

"I never wear feathers," Jane replied, "because I do not think that they would correspond with the condition in life of an artist's daughter who is going about on foot."

"But were you in a different situation in life, would you then wear feathers?"

"I do not know what I should do in that case. I attach very slight importance to such trifles. I merely consider what is suitable for myself, and should be very sorry to judge of others by the superficial information afforded by their dress."

M. Phlippon now began to advance rapidly in a career of dissipation. Jane did everything in her power to lure him to love his home. All her efforts were unavailing. Her situation was now painful in the extreme. Her mother, who had been the guardian angel of her life, was sleeping in the grave. The father was daily becoming more neglectful and unkind to his daughter. Under these circumstances, Jane, by the advice of friends, had resort to a legal process, by which there was secured to her, from the wreck of her mother's fortune, an annual income of about one hundred dollars.

In these gloomy hours which clouded the morning of her day, Jane found an unfailing resource and solace in her love of literature. With pen in hand, extracting beautiful passages and expanding suggested thoughts, she forgot her griefs and beguiled many hours, which would otherwise have been burdened with wretchedness.

Maria Antoinette, woe-worn and weary, in tones of despair uttered the exclamation:

"Oh! what a resource amid the casualties of life must there be in a highly cultivated mind."

The maiden could utter the same exclamation in accents of joy.

When Jane was in the convent, she became acquainted with a young lady from Amiens, Sophia Cannet. They formed for each other a strong attachment and commenced a correspondence which continued for many years. There was a gentleman in Amiens by the name of Roland de la Platière, born of an opulent family, and holding the quite important office of inspector of manufactures. His time was mainly occupied in travelling and study. Being deeply interested in all subjects relating to political economy, he had devoted much attention to that science, and had written several treatises upon commerce, mechanics and agriculture which had given him, in the literary and scientific world, no little celebrity. He frequently visited the father of Sophia. She often spoke to him of her friend Jane, showed him her portrait, and read to him extracts from her glowing letters. The calm philosopher became very much interested in the enthusiastic maiden, and entreated Sophia to give him a letter of introduction to her, upon one of his annual visits to Paris. Sophia had also often written to Jane of her father's friend, whom she regarded with so much reverence.

Jane, the enthusiastic, romantic Jane, saw in the serene philosopher one of the sages of antiquity, and almost literally bowed and worshipped. All the sentiments of M. Roland were in accordance with the most cherished emotions which glowed in her mind. She found what she had ever been seeking, but had never found before, a truly sympathetic soul. She looked up to M. Roland as to a superior being—to an oracle, by whose decisions she could judge whether her own opinions were right or wrong. It is true that M. Roland never entered those airy realms of beauty and regions of romance where Jane loved, at times, to revel. And perhaps Jane venerated him still more for his more stern and unimaginative philosophy. But his meditative wisdom, his abstraction from the frivolous pursuits of life, his high ambition, his elevated pleasures, his consciousness of superiority over the mass of his fellowmen, and his sleepless desire to be a benefactor of humanity, were all traits of character which resistlessly attracted the admiration of Jane. She adored him as a disciple adores his master. She listened eagerly to all his words, and loved communion with his thoughts. M. Roland was by no means insensible to this homage, and he was charmed with her society because she was so delighted with his own conversation. Several years after their acquaintance began M. Roland made an avowal of his attachment. Jane knew very well the pride of the Roland family, and that her worldly circumstances were such that the connection would not seem an advantageous one. She also was too proud to enter into a family who might feel dishonoured by the alliance. She, therefore, frankly told him that she felt much honoured by his addresses, and that she esteemed him more highly than any other man she had met. Her father was a ruined man, however, and by his increasing debts and his errors still deeper disgrace might be entailed upon all connected with him, and she could not think of allowing M. Roland to make his generosity to her a source of future mortification to himself.

The more she manifested this elevation of soul, in which Jane was perfectly sincere, the more earnestly did M. Roland persist in his plea. At last Jane, influenced by his entreaties, consented that he should make proposals to her father. He wrote to M. Phlippon. In reply he received an insulting letter, containing a blunt refusal. M. Phlippon declared that he had no idea of having for a son-in-law a man of such rigid principles, who would ever be reproaching him for all his little errors. He also told his daughter that she would find in a man of such austere virtue not a companion and an equal, but a tyrant. Jane laid this refusal of her father deeply to heart, and resolved that if she could not marry the man of her choice, she would marry no one else. She wrote to M. Roland, requesting him to abandon his design, and not to expose himself to any further affronts. She then requested permission of her father to retire to a convent.

The scanty income she had saved from her mother's property rendered it necessary for her to live with the utmost frugality. She determined to regulate her expenses in accordance with this small sum. Potatoes, rice, and beans, with a little salt, and occasionally the luxury of a little butter, were her only food. She allowed herself to leave the convent but twice a week: once, to call for an hour upon a relative, and once to visit her father, and look after his linen. She had a little room under the roof in the attic, where the pattering of the rain upon the tiles soothed and lulled her to sleep by night. She carefully secluded herself from association with the other inmates of the convent, receiving only a visit of an hour each evening from the much-loved Sister Agatha. Her time she devoted, with unremitting diligence to those literary avocations in which she found so much delight.

The quiet and seclusion of this life had many charms for Jane. Indeed, a person with such resource for enjoyment within herself could never be very weary. Several months thus glided away in tranquillity. She occasionally walked in the garden, at hours when no one else was there. The resignation, which she had so long cultivated; the peaceful conscience she enjoyed, in view of duty performed; the elevation of spirit which enabled her to rise superior to misfortune; the methodical arrangement of time, which assigned to each hour its appropriate duty; the habit of close application, which riveted her attention to her studies; the highly cultivated taste and buoyantly winged imagination, which opened before her all the fairy realms of fancy, were treasures which gilded her cell and enriched her heart.

In the course of five or six months M. Roland again visited Paris, and called at the convent to see Jane. He saw her pale and pensive face behind a grating, and the sight of one who had suffered so much from her faithful love for him, and the sound of her voice, which ever possessed a peculiar charm, revived in his mind those impressions which had been somewhat fading away. He again renewed his offer and entreated her to allow the marriage ceremony at once to be performed. Jane, without much delay, yielded to his appeals. They were married in the winter of 1780. Jane was then twenty-five years of age. Her husband was twenty years her senior.

The first year of their marriage life they passed in Paris. It was to Madame Roland a year of great enjoyment. Her husband was publishing a work upon the arts, and she, with all the energy of her enthusiastic mind, entered into all his literary enterprises. With great care and accuracy she prepared his manuscripts for the press and corrected the proofs. She lived in the study with him, became the companion of all his thoughts, and his assistant in all labours. The only recreations in which she indulged, during the winter, were to attend a course of lectures upon natural history and botany. M. Roland had hired ready furnished lodgings. She, well instructed by her mother in domestic duties, observing that all kinds of cooking did not agree with him, took pleasure in preparing his food with her own hands. Her husband engrossed her whole time, and, being naturally rather austere and imperious, he secluded her from the society of others and monopolised all her capabilities of friendly feeling.

At the close of the year the couple went to Amiens and soon after was born a daughter, her only child, whom she nurtured with the most assiduous care. Her literary labours were, however, unremitted, and she still lived in the study with her books and her pen. M. Roland was writing several articles for an encyclopædia. She aided most efficiently in collecting the materials and arranging the matter. Indeed, she wielded a far more vigorous pen than he did. Her copiousness of language, her facility of expression and the play of her fancy, gave her the command of a very fascinating style; and M. Roland obtained the credit for many passages rich in diction and beautiful in imagery for which he was indebted to the glowing imagination of his wife. Frequent sickness of her husband alarmed her for his life. The tenderness with which she watched over him strengthened the tie which united them. He could not but love a young and beautiful wife so devoted to him. She could not but love one upon whom she was conferring such rich blessings. Their little daughter, Eudora, was a source of great delight to the fond parents, and Madame Roland took the deepest interest in the developments of her mind. The office of M. Roland was highly lucrative, and his literary projects successful. They remained in Amiens four years.

Later they retired to La Platière, the paternal estate of M. Roland, situated at the base of the mountains near Lyons in the valley of the Saône. It is a region solitary and wild, with rivulets meandering down from the mountains, fringed with willows and poplars, and threading their way through narrow, yet smooth and fertile meadows luxuriant with vineyards. A large, square stone house, with regular windows and a roof nearly flat, of red tiles constituted the comfortable, spacious and substantial mansion.

Her mode of life during the five calm and sunny years at La Platière must have been exceedingly attractive. She rose with the sun, devoted sundry attentions to her husband and child, and personally superintended the arrangements for breakfast, taking an affectionate pleasure in preparing her husband's frugal food with her own hands. That social meal being passed, M. Roland entered the library for his intellectual toil, taking with him for his silent companion the idolised little Eudora. She amused herself with her pencil or reading or other studies, which her father and mother superintended. Madame Roland, in the meantime devoted herself, with most systematic energy, to her domestic concerns. She was a perfect housekeeper and each morning all the interests of her family, from the cellar to the garret, passed under her eye. She superintended the preservation of the fruit, the sorting of the linen, and those other details of domestic life which engross the attention of a good housewife. The systematic division of time, which seemed to be an instinctive principle of her nature, enabled her to accomplish all this in two hours. She had faithful and devoted servants to do the work. The superintendence was all that was required. This genius to superintend and be the head, while others contribute the hands, is not the most common of human endowments. Madame Roland, having thus attended to her domestic concerns, laid aside those cares for the remainder of the day, and entered the study to join her husband in his labours there.

At the close of the literary labours of the morning Madame Roland met her guests at the dinner table. The labour of the day was then over. The repast was prolonged with social converse. After dinner they walked in the garden, sauntered through the vineyard and looked at the innumerable objects of interest which are ever to be found in the yard of a spacious farm. Madame Roland frequently retired to the library to write letters to her friends or to superintend the lessons of Eudora. Occasionally, of a fine day, she would walk for several miles, calling at the cottages of the peasantry, whom she greatly endeared to her by her unvarying kindness. In the evening, after tea, they again resorted to the library. Guests of distinguished name and influence were frequently with them, and the hours glided swiftly, cheered by the brilliance of philosophy and genius. The journals of the day were read, Madame Roland being usually called upon as reader. When not thus reading, she usually sat at her work-table, employing her fingers with her needle, while she took part in the conversation.

"This kind of life," says Madame Roland, "would be very austere, were not my husband a man of great merit, whom I love with my whole heart. I congratulate myself on enjoying it; and I exert my best endeavours to make it last."

Again she draws the captivating picture of rural pleasures:

"I am preserving pears which will be delicious. We are drying raisins and prunes. We overlook the servants busy in the vineyard; repose in the shady groves, and on the green meadows; gather walnuts from the trees; and having collected our stock of fruit for the winter, spread it to dry. After breakfast this morning we are all going in a body to gather almonds. Throw off, then, dear friend, your fetters for a while, and come and join us in our retreat. You will find here true friendship and real simplicity of heart."

*   *   *   *   *

Madame Roland was thus living at La Platière, in the enjoyment of all that this world can give of peace and happiness, when the first portentious mutterings of the French Revolution fell upon her ears. She eagerly caught the sounds, and, believing them the precursor of blessings, rejoiced in the assurance that the hour was approaching when long-oppressed humanity would reassert its rights and achieve its triumph. Little did she dream of the woes which in surging billows were to roll over her country and which were to engulf her and all whom she loved in their tide. Her faith in human nature was so strong that she could foresee no obstacles and no dangers in the way of immediate disfranchisement from all laws and usages which her judgment disapproved. Her whole soul was aroused and she devoted all her affections and every energy of her mind to the welfare of the human race.

Louis XVI. and Maria Antoinette had but recently inherited the throne of the Bourbons. Louis was benevolent, but destitute of the decision of character requisite to hold the reins of government in a stormy period. Maria Antoinette had neither culture of mind nor knowledge of the world. She was an amiable but spoiled child, with native nobleness of character, but with those defects which are the natural consequence of the frivolous education she had received. She thought never of duty and responsibility; always and only of pleasure. It was her misfortune rather than her fault that the idea never entered her mind that kings and queens had aught else to do than to indulge in luxury. It would be hardly possible to conceive of two characters less qualified to occupy the throne in stormy times than were Louis and Maria. The people were slowly, but with resistless power, rising against the abuses of the aristocracy and the monarchy. Louis, a man of unblemished kindness, was made the scapegoat for the sins of oppressive, profligate princes, who for centuries had trodden with iron hoofs upon the necks of their subjects. The accumulated hate of ages was poured upon his head.

The National Assembly consisted of the nobility, the higher clergy, and representatives, chosen by the people, from all parts of France.

M. Roland, who was quite an idol with the populace of Lyons and its vicinity, was chosen representative to the Assembly from the city of Lyons. In that busy city the revolutionary movement had begun with great power, and the name of Roland was the rallying point of the people now struggling to escape from oppression. M. Roland spent some time in the city, drawn thither by the intense interest of the times, and in the salon of Madame Roland meetings were every evening held by the most influential men of the revolutionary party. Her ardour stimulated their zeal, and her well-stored mind and fascinating eloquence guided their councils.

In this rising conflict between plebeian and patrician, between democrat and aristocrat, the position in which M. Roland and wife were placed, as most conspicuous and influential members of the revolutionary party, arrayed against them, with daily increasing animosity, the aristocratic community of Lyons. Each day their names were pronounced by the advocates of reform with more enthusiasm and by their opponents with deepening hostility. The applause and the censure alike invigorated Madame Roland, and her whole soul became absorbed in the idea of popular liberty. This object became her passion, and she devoted herself to it with the concentration of every energy of mind and heart.

On the 20th of February, 1791, Madame Roland accompanied her husband to Paris, as he took his seat in the National Assembly. Her persuasive influence was dictating those measures which were driving the ancient nobility of France from their châteaux, and her vigorous mind was guiding those blows before which the throne of the Bourbons trembled. The unblemished and incorruptible integrity of M. Roland, his simplicity of manners and ability, invested him immediately with much authority among his associates. The brilliance of his wife also reflected much lustre upon his name. Madame Roland with her growing zeal, had just written a pamphlet upon the new order of things, in language so powerful and impressive that more than sixty thousand copies had been sold—an enormous number, considering the comparative fewness of readers at that time. She, of course, was received with the most flattering attention, and great deference was paid to her opinions. She attended daily the sittings of the Assembly, and listened with the deepest interest to the debates.

All her tastes were with the ancient nobility and their defenders. All her principles were with the people. And as she contrasted the unrefined exterior and clumsy speech of the democratic leaders with the courtly bearing and elegant diction of those who rallied around the throne, she was aroused to a more vehement desire for the elevation of those with whom she had cast in her lot. The conflict with the nobles was of short continuance. The energy of rising democracy soon vanquished them.

The most moderate party was called the Girondist. It was so called because their most prominent leaders were from the department of the Gironde. They would deprive the King of many of his prerogatives, but not of his crown. They would take from him his despotic power, but not his life. They would raise the mass of the people to the enjoyment of liberty, but to liberty controlled by vigorous law. Opposed to them were the Jacobins—far more radical in their reform. They would break down all privileged orders, confiscate the property of the nobles and place prince and beggar on the footing of equality. These were the two great parties into which revolutionary France was divided and the conflict between them was the most fierce and implacable earth has ever witnessed.

M. Roland and wife gathered around them every evening many of the most influential members of the Assembly. They attached themselves with all their zeal and energy to the Girondists. Four evenings of every week the leaders of this party met in the salon of Madame Roland, to deliberate respecting their measures.

The powerful influence which Madame Roland was thus exerting could not be concealed. She appeared to have no ambition for personal renown. She sought only to elevate the position and expand the celebrity of her husband. It was whispered from ear to ear, and now and then openly asserted in the Assembly, that the bold and decisive measures of the Girondists received their impulse from the lovely wife of M. Roland. She also furnished many very able articles for a widely circulated journal, established by the Girondists for the advocacy of their political views.

The spirit of the revolution was advancing with giant strides, and the throne was reeling beneath the blows of the people. Massacres were rife all over the kingdom. The sky was nightly illumined by conflagrations. Nobles were abandoning their estates and escaping from perils and death to refuge in the little army of emigrants at Coblentz. The King, insulted and a prisoner, reigned but in name. He hoped, by the appointment of a Republican ministry to pacify the democratic spirit.

He yielded to the pressure, dismissed his ministers, and surrendered himself to the Girondists for the appointment of a new ministry. The Girondists called upon M. Roland to take the important post of Minister of the Interior. It was a perilous position to fill, but what danger will not ambition face? In the present posture of affairs the Minister of the Interior was the monarch of France. M. Roland smiled nervously at the power which, thus unsolicited, was passing into his hands. Madame Roland, whose all-absorbing passion it now was to elevate her husband to the highest summits of greatness, was gratified in view of the honour and agitated in view of the peril; but, to her exalted spirit, the greater the danger, the more heroic the act.

"The burden is heavy," she said; "but Roland has a great consciousness of his own powers, and would derive fresh strength from the feeling of being useful to liberty and his country."

In March, 1792, he entered upon his arduous and exalted office. When M. Roland made his first appearance at court instead of arraying himself in the court dress, he affected in his costume the simplicity of his principles. He had not forgotten the impression produced in France by Franklin, as in republican simplicity he moved among the glittering throng at Versailles. He accordingly presented himself at the Tuileries in a plain black coat, with a round hat, and dusty shoes fastened with ribbons instead of buckles. The courtiers were indignant. The King was highly displeased at what he considered an act of disrespect. The master of ceremonies was in consternation, and exclaimed with a look of horror to General Damuriez:

"My dear sir, he has not even buckles on his shoes!"

"Mercy upon us!" exclaimed the old general, with the most laughable expression of affected gravity, "we shall then all go to ruin together!"

M. Roland after his first interview with the monarch assured his wife that the community had formed a totally erroneous estimate of the King; that he was a hearty supporter of the Constitution which had been forced upon him. The prompt reply of Madame Roland displayed even more than her characteristic sagacity:

"If Louis is sincerely a friend of the Constitution, he must be virtuous beyond the common race of mortals. Mistrust your own virtue, M. Roland. You are only an honest countryman wandering amid a crowd of courtiers. They speak our language; we do not know theirs. No! Louis cannot love the chains that fetter him. He may feign to caress them. He thinks only of how he can spurn them. No man likes his humiliation. Trust in human nature; that never deceives. Distrust courts. Your virtue is too elevated to see the snares which courtiers spread beneath your feet."

From all the spacious apartments of the mansion alloted as the residence of the Minister of the Interior Madame Roland selected a small and retired parlour, which she had furnished with every attraction as a library and a study. This was her much-loved retreat, and here M. Roland, in the presence of his wife, was accustomed to see his friends in all their confidential intercourse. But the position of the Girondists began to be more and more perilous. The army of emigrant nobles at Coblentz, within the dominions of the King of Prussia, was rapidly increasing in numbers. There were hundreds of thousands in France, the most illustrious in rank and opulence, who would join such an army.

The people all believed that Louis wished to escape from Paris and head that army. On the other hand, they saw another party, the Jacobin, noisy, turbulent, sanguinary and threatening with destruction all connected in any way with the execrated throne. M. Roland was urged to present to the throne a most earnest letter of expostulation and advice. Madame Roland sat down at her desk and wrote the letter for her husband. It was expressed in that glowing style so eminently at her command. Its eloquence was inspired by the foresight she had of impending perils. M. Roland, almost trembling in view of its boldness and its truths, presented the letter to the King. Its last sentences will give some idea of its character:

Love, serve the Revolution, and the people will love it and serve it in you. Ratify the measures to extirpate their fanaticism. Paris trembles in view of its danger. Surround its walls with an army of defence. Delay longer, and you will be deemed a conspirator and an accomplice. Just Heaven! hast thou stricken kings with blindness? I know that truth is rarely welcomed at the foot of thrones. I know, too, that the withholding of truth from kings renders revolutions so often necessary. As a citizen, a minister, I owe truth to the King, and nothing shall prevent me from making it reach his ear.

This celebrated letter was presented to the King on the 11th of June, 1792. On the same day M. Roland received a letter from the King informing him that he was dismissed from office.

"Here am I, dismissed from office," was M. Roland's exclamation to his wife on his return home.

"Present your letter to the Assembly, that the nation may see for what counsel you have been dismissed," replied the undaunted wife.

M. Roland did so. He was received as a martyr to patriotism. The letter was read amid the loudest applause. It was ordered to be printed and circulated by tens of thousands through the kingdom; and there came rolling back upon the metropolis the echo of the most tumultuous indignation and applause. The famous letter was read by all France—nay, more, by all Europe.

Roland was a hero. Upon this wave of enthusiastic popularity Madame Roland and her husband retired from the magnificent palace where they had dwelt for so short a time and selected for their retreat very humble apartments in an apparently obscure street.

But M. Roland and wife were more powerful now than ever before. The letter had placed them in the front ranks of the friends of reform, and enshrined them in the hearts of the ever fickle populace. Even the Jacobins were compelled to swell the universal voice of commendation. M. Roland's apartments were ever thronged. All important plans were discussed and shaped by him and his wife before they were presented to the Assembly.

The outcry against M. Roland's dismissal was falling in thunder tones on the ear of the King. This act had fanned those flames of revolutionary frenzy which were now glaring in every part of France. The people, intoxicated and maddened by the discovery of their power, were now arrayed, with irresistible thirstings for destruction and blood, against the King, the court, and the nobility. There was no hope for Louis but in the recall of M. Roland. The Jacobins were upon him in locust legions. M. Roland alone could bring the Girondists, as a shield, between the throne and the mob. He was recalled, and again moved in calm triumph from his obscure chambers to the palace of the minister. If Madame Roland's letter dismissed him from office, her letter also restored him again with an enormous accumulation of power.

Madame Roland was far more conscious of the peril than her husband. With intense emotion, but calmly and firmly, she looked upon the gathering storm. The peculiarity of her character, and her great moral courage, was illustrated by the mode of life she vigorously adopted. She was entirely undazzled, and resolved that, consecrating all her energies to the demands of the tempestuous times, she would waste no time in fashionable parties and heartless visits. Selecting for her own use one of the smallest parlours, she furnished it as her library. Here she lived engrossed in study, busy with her pen, and taking an unseen but most active part in all those measures which were literally agitating the whole civilised world. Her little library was the sanctuary for all confidential conversation upon matters of state. Here her husband met his political friends to mature their measures. She wrote many of his proclamations, his letters, his state papers, and with all the glowing fervour of an enthusiastic woman.

She writes:

Without me my husband would have been quite as good a minister, for his knowledge, his activity, his integrity were all his own; but with me he attracted more attention, because I infused into his writings that mixture of spirit and gentleness, of authoritative reason and seducing sentiment, which is, perhaps, only to be found in the language of a woman who has a clear head and a feeling heart.

Anarchy now reigned throughout France. The King and the royal family were imprisoned in the Temple. The Girondists in the National Convention, and M. Roland at the head of the ministry, were struggling to restore the dominion of law, and, if possible, to save the life of the King. The Jacobins, who, unable to resist the popularity of M. Roland, had, for a time, coöperated with the Girondists, now began to separate themselves again more widely from them. They flattered the mob. They encouraged every possible demonstration of lawless violence. In tones daily increasing in boldness and efficiency, they declared the Girondists to be the friends of the monarch, and the enemies of popular liberty.

Madame Roland, in the name of her husband, drew up for the Convention the plan of a republic as a substitute for the throne. From childhood she had yearned for a republic. Now the throne and hereditary rank were virtually abolished, and all France clamoured for a republic. Her husband was nominally Minister of the Interior, but his power was gone. The mob of Paris had usurped the place of King, and Constitution and law. The Jacobins were attaining the decided ascendency. The guillotine was daily crimsoned with the blood of the noblest citizens of

France. The streets and the prisons were polluted with the massacre of the innocent.

M. Roland was almost frantic in view of these horrors which he had no power to quell. The mob, headed by the Jacobins, had now the complete ascendency, and he was minister but in name. He urged the adoption of immediate and energetic measures to arrest these execrable deeds of lawless violence. Many of the Girondists in the Assembly gave vehement utterance to their execration of the massacres. Others were intimidated by the weapons which the Jacobins were now so effectually wielding. Madame Roland distinctly saw and deeply felt the peril to which she and her friends were exposed. She knew, and they all knew, that defeat was death.

The question between the Girondist and the Jacobin was: "Who shall lie down on the guillotine?" For some time the issue of the struggle was uncertain. The Jacobins summoned their allies, the mob. They surrounded the doors and the windows of the Assembly, and with their howlings sustained their friends. The Girondists found themselves, at the close of the struggle, defeated, yet not so decidedly but that they still clung to hope.

M. Roland, who had not yet entirely lost, with the people, that popularity which swept him again into the office of Minister of the Interior, now presented to the Assembly his resignation of power which was merely nominal. Great efforts had for some time been made by his adversaries, to turn the tide of popular hatred against him, and especially against his wife. Madame Roland might have fled from these perils, and have retired with her husband to tranquillity and safety, but she urged M. Roland to remain at his post and resolved to remain herself and meet her destiny, whatever it might be.

The Jacobins now made a direct and infamous attempt to turn the rage of the populace against Madame Roland. She was summoned to present herself before the Convention, to confront her accuser, and defend herself from the scaffold. Her gentle yet imperial spirit was undaunted by the magnitude of the peril. Her name had often been mentioned in the Assembly as the inspiring genius of the most influential party which had risen up amid the storms of the Revolution. Her talents, her accomplishments, her fascinating eloquence, had spread her renown widely through Europe.

The aspect of a woman combining in her person and mind all the attractions of nature and genius, entering this vast assembly of irritated men to speak in defence of her life, at once hushed the clamour of hoarse voices and subdued the rage of angry disputants. Silence filled the hall. Every eye was fixed upon her. She stood before the bar.

"What is your name?" inquired the president.

She paused for a moment, and then in clear and liquid tones answered:

"Roland! A name of which I am proud, for it is that of a good and an honourable man."

"Do you know Achille Viard?" the president inquired.

"I have once, and but once, seen him."

"What has passed between you?"

"Twice he has written to me, soliciting an interview. Once I saw him. After a short conversation, I perceived that he was a spy, and dismissed him with the contempt he deserved."

Briefly, in tremulous tones of voice, but with a spirit of firmness which no terrors could daunt, she entered upon her defence. It was the first time that a woman's voice had been heard in the midst of the clamour of these enraged combatants. The Assembly, unused to such a scene, were fascinated by her attractive eloquence. Madame Roland was acquitted by acclamation. Upon the spot the president proposed that the marked respect of the Convention be conferred upon Madame Roland. With enthusiasm the resolution was carried. As she retired from the hall, her bosom glowing with the excitement of the triumph she had won, her ear was greeted with the enthusiastic applause of the whole Assembly. The eyes of all France had been attracted to her as she thus defended herself and her friends, and confounded her enemies.

The most distressing embarrassments now surrounded M. Roland. He could not abandon power without abandoning himself and his supporters in the Assembly to the guillotine; and while continuing in power, he was compelled to witness deeds of atrocity from which not only his soul revolted, but to which it was necessary for him apparently to give his sanction. Thus situated, he sent in his final resignation and retired to humble lodgings in one of the obscure streets of Paris. Here, anxiously watching the progress of events, he began to make preparations to leave the mob-enthralled metropolis and seek a retreat in the calm seclusion of La Platière. Neither the sacredness of law nor the weapons of their friends could longer afford them any protection. The danger became so imminent that the friends of Madame Roland brought her the dress of a peasant girl, and entreated her to put it on, as a disguise and escape by night, that her husband might follow after her, unencumbered by his family; but she proudly repelled that which she deemed a cowardly artifice. She threw the dress aside, exclaiming:

"I am ashamed to resort to any such expedient. I will neither disguise myself, nor make any attempt at secret escape. My enemies may find me always in my place. If I am assassinated it shall be in my own home. I owe my country an example of firmness, and I will give it."

The gray of a dull and sombre morning was just beginning to appear as Madame Roland threw herself upon a bed for a few moments of repose. Overwhelmed by sorrow and fatigue, she had just fallen asleep, when a band of armed men rudely broke into her house, and demanded to be conducted to her apartment. She knew too well the object of the summons. The order for her arrest was presented her. She calmly read it, and requested permission to write to a friend. The request was granted. When the note was finished, the officer informed her that it would be necessary for him to be made acquainted with its contents. She quietly tore it into fragments and cast it into the fire. Then, imprinting her last kiss upon the cheek of her unconscious child, with the composure which such a catastrophe would naturally produce in so heroic a mind, she left her home for the prison. As she was led from the house a vast crowd collected around the door, who, believing her to be a traitor to her country, and in league with her enemies, shouted, "A la guillotine!" Unmoved by their cries, she looked calmly without gesture or reply. One of the officers, to relieve her from the insults to which she was exposed, asked her if she wished to have the windows of the carriage closed.

"No!" she replied, "I do not fear the looks of honest men, and I brave those of my enemies."

"You have very great resolution," was the reply, "thus calmly to await justice."

"Justice!" she exclaimed; "were justice done I should not be here. But I shall go to the scaffold as fearlessly as I now proceed to the prison."

At ten o'clock that evening, her cell being prepared, she entered it for the first time. It was a cold, bare room, with walls blackened by the dust and damp of ages. There was a small fireplace in the room, and a narrow window, with a double iron grating, which admitted but a dim twilight even at noonday. In one corner there was a pallet of straw. The chill night air crept in at the unglazed window, and the dismal tocsin proclaimed that Paris was still the scene of tumult and of violence. Madame Roland threw herself upon her humble bed, and was so overpowered by fatigue and exhaustion that she woke not from her dreamless slumber until twelve o'clock of the next day.

Eudora, who had been left by her mother in the care of weeping domestics, was taken by a friend and watched over and protected with maternal care. Though Madame Roland never saw her idolised child again, her heart was comforted in the prison by the assurance that she had found a home with those who, for her mother's sake, would love and cherish her.

When Madame Roland awoke from her long sleep, instead of yielding to despair and surrendering herself to useless repinings, she immediately began to arrange her cell as comfortably as possible, and to look round for such sources of comfort and enjoyment as might yet be obtained. She obtained the favour of a small table, and then of a neat white spread to cover it. This she placed near the window to serve for her writing-desk. To keep this table, which she prized so highly, unsoiled, she smilingly told her keeper that she should make a dining-table of her stove. A rusty dining-table indeed it was. Two hairpins, which she drew from her own clustering ringlets, she drove into a shelf for pegs to hang her clothes upon. These arrangements she made as cheerfully as when superintending the disposition of the gorgeous furniture in the palace over which she had presided. Having thus provided her study, her next care was to obtain a few books. She happened to have Thomson's "Seasons," a favourite volume of hers, in her pocket. Through the jailer's wife she succeeded in obtaining "Plutarch's Lives" and Sheridan's "Dictionary."

The prison regulations were very severe. The Government allowed twenty pence per day for the support of each prisoner. Ten pence was to be paid to the jailer for the furniture he put into the cell; tenpence only remained for food. The prisoners were, however, allowed to purchase such food as they pleased from their own purse. Madame Roland, with that stoicism which enabled her to triumph over all ordinary ills, resolved to conform to the prison allowance. She took bread and water alone for breakfast. The dinner was coarse meat and vegetables. The money she saved by this great frugality she distributed among the poorer prisoners. The only indulgence she allowed herself was in the purchase of books and flowers. In reading and with her pen she beguiled the weary days of her imprisonment. And though at times her spirit was overwhelmed with anguish at her desolate home and blighted hopes, she still found solace in the warm affections which sprang up around her, even in the uncongenial atmosphere of a prison.

One day some commissioners called at her cell, hoping to extort from her the secret of her husband's retreat. She looked them calmly in the face and said:

"Gentlemen, I know perfectly well where my husband is. I scorn to tell you a lie. I know, also, my own strength. And I assure you that there is no earthly power which can induce me to betray him."

The commissioners withdrew, admiring her heroism, and convinced that she was still able to wield an influence which might yet bring the guillotine upon their own necks. Her doom was sealed. Her heroism was a crime. She was too illustrious to live.

✻ ✻ ✻ ✻ ✻

Madame Roland remained some time in the Abbayé prison. On the twenty-fourth day of her imprisonment, to her inexpressible astonishment, an officer entered her cell, and informed her that she was liberated, as no charge could be found against her. Hardly crediting her senses—fearing that she should wake up and find her freedom but a dream—she took a coach and hastened to her own door. Her eyes were full of tears of joy and her heart almost bursting with delight, in the anticipation of again pressing her idolised child to her bosom. Her hand was upon the door latch—she had not yet passed the threshold— when two men, who had watched at the door of her dwelling, again seized her in the name of the law. In spite of her tears and supplications, they conveyed her to the prison of St. Pélagié. This loathsome receptacle of crime was filled with the abandoned who had been swept from the streets of Paris. It was, apparently, a studied humiliation, to compel their victim to associate with beings from whom her soul shrank with loathing.

Many hours of every day she beguiled in this prison in writing the memoirs of her own life. It was an eloquent and a touching narrative, written with the expectation that each sentence might be interrupted by the entrance of the executioners to conduct her to trial and to the guillotine. In this unveiling of the heart to the world, one sees a noble nature animated to benevolence by native generosity. The consciousness of spiritual elevation constituted her only solace. The anticipation of a lofty reputation after death was her only heaven. No one can read the thoughts she penned but with the deepest emotion.

The Girondists who had been in prison were led from their dungeons in the Conciergerie to their execution on October 31, 1793. Upon that very day Madame Roland was conveyed from the prison of St. Pélagié to the same gloomy cells vacated by the death of her friends. She was cast into a bare and miserable dungeon, in that receptacle of woe, where there was not even a bed. Another prisoner, moved with compassion, drew his own pallet into her cell, that she might not be compelled to throw herself for repose upon the cold, wet stones. The chill air of winter had now come, and yet no covering was allowed her. Through the long night she shivered with the cold.

* * * * *

The day after Madame Roland was placed in the Conciergerie, she was visited by one of the officers of the revolutionary party, and closely questioned concerning the friendship she had entertained for the Girondists. She frankly avowed the affection with which she cherished their memory, but she declared that she and they were the cordial friends of republican liberty; that they wished to preserve, not to destroy, the Constitution. The examination lasted for three hours, and consisted in an incessant torrent of criminations, to which she was hardly permitted to offer one word in reply. This examination taught her the nature of the accusations which would be brought against her. She sat down in her cell that very night, and, with a rapid pen, sketched that defence which has been pronounced one of the most eloquent and touching monuments of the Revolution. It so beautifully illustrates the heroism of her character and the beauty and energy of her mind that it will ever be read with the liveliest interest.

She remained in the Conciergerie but one week, and during that time so endeared herself to all as to become the prominent object of attention and love. Her case is one of the most extraordinary the history of the world has presented, in which the very highest degree of heroism is combined with the most resistless loveliness. With an energy of will, an inflexibility of purpose, a firmness of endurance which no mortal man has ever exceeded, she combined gentleness and tenderness and affection.

The day before her trial, her advocate, Chauveau de la Garde, visited her to consult respecting her defence. She, well aware that no one could speak a word in her favour but at the peril of his own life, and also fully conscious that her doom was already sealed, drew a ring from her finger, and said to him:

"To-morrow I shall be no more. I know the fate which awaits me. Your kind assistance cannot avail aught for me, and would but endanger you. I pray you, therefore, not to come to the tribunal, but to accept of this last testimony of my regard."

The next day she was led to her trial. She attired herself in a white robe, as a symbol of her innocence, and her long dark hair fell in thick curls on her neck and shoulders. She emerged from her dungeon a vision of unusual loveliness. The prisoners who were walking in the corridors gathered around her, and with smiles and words of encouragement she infused energy into their hearts. Calm and invincible she met her judges. Whenever she attempted to utter a word in her defence, she was browbeaten by the judges, and silenced by the clamours of the mob which filled the tribunal. At last the president demanded of her that she should reveal her husband's asylum. She proudly replied:

"I do not know of any law by which I can be obliged to violate the strongest feelings of nature."

This was sufficient, and she was immediately condemned. Her sentence was thus expressed:

The public accuser has drawn up the present indictment against Jane Mary Phlippon, the wife of Roland, late Minister of the Interior, for having wickedly and designedly aided and assisted in the conspiracy which existed against the unity and indivisibility of the Republic, against the liberty and safety of the French people, by assembling, at her house, in secret council, the principal chiefs of that conspiracy, and by keeping up a correspondence tending to facilitate their treasonable designs. The tribunal, having heard the public accuser deliver his reasons concerning the application of the law, condemns Jane Mary Phlippon, wife of Roland, to the punishment of death.

She listened calmly to her sentence, and then, rising, bowed with dignity to her judges and, smiling, said:

"I thank you, gentlemen, for thinking me worthy of sharing the fate of the great men whom you have assassinated. I shall endeavour to imitate their firmness on the scaffold."

With the buoyant step of a child, and with a rapidity which almost betokened joy, she passed beneath the narrow portal, and descended to her cell, from which she was to be led, with the morning light, to death. The prisoners had assembled to greet her on her return, and anxiously gathered round her. She looked upon them with a smile of perfect tranquillity, and, drawing her hand across her neck, made a sign expressive of her doom.

The morning of the 8th of November, 1793, dawned gloomily upon Paris. It was one of the darkest days of that reign of terror which, for so long a period, enveloped France in its sombre shades. The ponderous gates of the courtyard of the Conciergerie opened that morning to a long procession of carts loaded with victims for the guillotine. Madame Roland had contemplated her fate too long, and had disciplined her spirit too severely, to fail of fortitude in this last hour of trial. She came from her cell scrupulously attired. A serene smile was upon her cheeks, and the glow of joyous animation lighted up her features as she waved an adieu to the weeping prisoners who gathered round her. The last cart was assigned to Madame Roland. She entered it with a step as light and elastic as if it were a carriage for a morning's drive. By her side stood an infirm old man, M. La Marche. He was pale and trembling, and his fainting heart, in view of the approaching terror, almost ceased to beat. She sustained him by her arm, and addressed to him words of consolation and encouragement, in cheerful accents and with a benignant smile. She stood firmly in the cart, looking with a serene eye upon the crowds which lined the streets, and listening to the clamour which filled the air. A crowd surrounded the cart shouting:

"To the guillotine! to the guillotine!"

She looked kindly upon them, and bending over the railing of the cart, said to them in tones as placid as if she were addressing her own child:

"My friends, I *am* going to the guillotine. In a few moments I shall be there. They who send me thither will ere long follow me. I go innocent. They will come stained with blood. You who now applaud our execution will then applaud theirs with equal zeal."

The long procession arrived at the guillotine, and the bloody work began. The victims were dragged from the carts, and the axe rose and fell with unceasing rapidity. Head after head fell into the basket. The executioners approached the cart where Madame Roland stood by the side of her fainting companion. With an animated countenance and a cheerful smile, she was endeavouring to infuse fortitude into his soul. The executioner grasped her by the arm.

"Stay," said she, slightly resisting his grasp; "I have one favour to ask, and that is not for myself. I beseech you grant it me." Then turning to the old man she said: "Do you precede me to the scaffold. To see my blood flow would make you suffer the bitterness of death twice over. I must spare you the pain of witnessing my execution."

The stern officer gave a surly refusal, replying: "My orders are to take you first."

With that winning smile and that fascinating grace which were almost resistless, she rejoined: "You cannot, surely, refuse a woman her last request."

The hard-hearted executor of the law was brought within the influence of her enchantment. He paused, looked at her for a moment in bewilderment, and yielded. The poor old man, more dead than alive, was conducted upon the scaffold and placed beneath the fatal axe. Madame Roland, without the slightest change of colour, or the apparent tremor of a nerve, saw the ponderous instrument, with its glittering edge, glide upon its deadly mission, and the decapitated trunk of her friend was thrown aside to give place for her. With a placid countenance and a buoyant step she ascended the steps. She stood for a moment upon the platform, looked calmly around upon the vast concourse, and then bowing before a clay statue of Liberty near by exclaimed: "O Liberty! what crimes are committed in thy name." She surrendered herself to the executioner, and was bound to the plank. The plank fell to its horizontal position, bringing her head under the fatal axe. The glittering steel glided through the groove, and the head of Madame Roland was severed from her body.

The grief of M. Roland, when apprised of the event, was unbounded. For a time he entirely lost his senses. Life to him was no longer endurable. Privately he left by night, the kind friends who had concealed him for six months, and wandered to such a distance from his asylum as to secure his protectors from any danger on his account. Through the long hours of the winter's night he continued his dreary walk, till the first gray of the morning appeared. Drawing a long stiletto from the inside of his walking-stick, he placed the head of it against the trunk of a tree, and threw himself upon the sharp weapon. The point pierced his heart and he fell lifeless upon the frozen ground. Some peasants passing by discovered his body. A piece of paper was pinned to the breast of his coat, upon which there were written these words:

Whoever thou art that findest these remains, respect them as those of a virtuous man. After hearing of my wife's death, I would not stay another day in a world so stained with crime.

The daughter of Madame Roland succeeded in escaping the fury of the tyrants of the Revolution. She lived surrounded by kind protectors, and in subsequent years was married to M. Champeneaux, the son of one of her mother's intimate friends.

XI

GRACE DARLING

Grace Darling was born on the 24th of November, 1815, at a small town upon the northeastern coast of England. She was the seventh child of her parents. Her grandfather, Robert Darling, had been keeper of the coal-light on the outmost of the Farne Islands, and her father, William, succeeded him in that post. In 1826, however, when Grace was eleven years old, William Darling took his family to Longstone, another island of the same group.

These Farne Islands are about twenty-five in number at low tide, and, as a visitor has pointed out, are desolate to an uncommon degree, although they are at no great distance from the Northumberland coast. The sea rushes with great force through the channels between the islands. Longstone, upon which Grace dwelt was, says another visitor, of dark whinstone, cracked in every direction and worn with the action of winds, waves and tempests, since the world began. Over the greater part of it was not a blade of grass nor a grain of earth; it was hard and iron-like stone, crusted round all the coast as far as high water-mark with limpet and still smaller shells. We ascended wrinkled hills of black stone, and descended into worn and dismal dells of the same, into some of which, where the tide got entrance, it came pouring and roaring in raging whiteness, and churning the loose fragments of whinstone into round pebbles, and piling them up in deep crevices, with seaweed. Over our heads screamed hundreds of hovering birds, the gull mingling its hideous laughter most wildly.

Fancy a lone lighthouse standing upon this pile of stone, dropped seemingly, in the midst of the water, five miles from the mainland. The sea tosses, and swells, and beats the rocks unceasingly. In fine weather it is blue and more kindly; in storms the waters are black and furious and fearful. It was known as a most desolate and dangerous lighthouse, and its service could be only a man and family of courage, endurance, large human feeling and strong sense of duty.

In such an abode grew the little girl, almost alone so far as school friends go. Her father taught her to read and write together with the seven of her brothers and sisters, and their schoolroom was the lantern of the lighthouse. Her instructors were in other ways the sky and the breaking surf; her comrades the sea birds and the simple shell fish and floating grasses of the salt water and all the strange and curious growths the sea brings wherever it is free.

Like her brothers and sisters, Grace was schooled after the simpler fashion. But when such days were passed she kept to her home rather than go out into the world or marry. The lighthouse sheltered a united and happy family. Grace loved the seclusion of that life and assisted her mother with the work of the household. Others of the daughters had gone to homes of their own upon the mainland.

If our surroundings help to form our characters, here in this lighthouse Grace must have grown into a strong self-control and a spirit of helpfulness toward hapless people and those wrecks upon the Farne Islands, of which many a legend has been told.

About thirty years before she was born a fine merchantman from America had struck the ledges near the lighthouse, and it is said that to the recital of this ship-wreck, of how the brave sailors fought for life and how one by one they fell or were swept into the fierce waters, the little girl would listen weeping, and then go pitifully to her bed. This tale, and the story of other sea mishaps, had a special attraction for the child, and the strength of her interest and compassion for the shipwrecked were noticed by her family as they sat round the family table of an evening, knitting, talking of the sea and watching the bright beacon above.

So it was that Grace Darling grew to womanhood. She was twenty-two years old when the disaster came that made evident what sort of a girl had come to woman's years upon the solitary island.

In the fall of the year, 1838, one fifth of September, a steamer, called the *Forfarshire*, a vessel of small size, but laden with a considerable cargo, sailed for Dundee, Scotland, from the port of Hull, England. There were forty-one passengers and twenty-two of the crew—sixty-three in all. The ship was but two years old, but her boilers were in bad order, although they had had some overhauling before she cleared her port.

She sailed in the early evening and for a part of her way seemed to be steaming safely. But as the vessel neared Flamborough Head the captain and crew became disturbed by many anxieties. Word passed from mouth to mouth among the passengers that the leak of the boiler was growing rapidly and the firemen could with difficulty keep up the fires. So much did this delay the passage of the steamer that toward the evening of the following day she had only made the channel between the coast and the Farne Islands. The wind was blowing from the north. It is reported that the engines became utterly useless. There being great danger of drifting ashore, the sails were hoisted fore and aft, and the vessel got about in order to get her before the wind and keep her off the land. It rained heavily during the entire time, and the fog was so dense that it became impossible to tell the situation of the vessel. At length breakers were discovered close to leeward, and the Farne Light, which about the same period became visible, left no doubt as to the peril of all on board.

Passengers crowded the deck and as rain beat upon them and the fog shut out all but the sad scene on board, friends and strangers pressed hands for support and sought hopeful words from one another's lips. The sails hoisted for a defence became useless for the purpose, the wind was rising to tempest strength, and all control over the vessel seemed gone. The sea was master and was tossing the helpless steamer in its waves, and, as the summer wind drives thistledown in its course, was driving her toward the light. The billows beat upon the frail timbers and every lurch and swell took the vessel nearer the island where the wild waters were breaking in foam.

At length appeared in an opening of the fog a great rock, frightfully rugged, deadly to a ship weakened and in the power of the sea. Passengers and crew alike knew the spot, and they knew that unless some miracle prevailed the ship must go to pieces. There was a moment's delay, the sea seemed putting off its final victory, and then it brought the vessel with her bow foremost upon the rocks.

A panic followed. All who had been below rushed to the deck and sought in the companionship of wretchedness an escape from threatening destruction. Some of the crew, determined to save themselves, lowered the larboard quarter boat, and left the ship. The boiling sea now swept over the decks.

Very soon after the first shock a powerful wave struck the vessel on the quarter, and raising her off the rocks allowed her immediately after to fall violently upon it, the sharp edge striking her amidships. She was by this fairly broken in two pieces, and the after part, containing the cabin with many passengers was instantly carried off through a tremendous current, called the Piper Gut. The captain and his wife were among those who perished.

The forepart still remained crushed upon the rocks. Upon its deck were eight unfortunate creatures—five sailors and three of the passengers. In the cabin below lay a woman huddling two children in her arms, a girl of eleven and a boy of eight. The waves washed through the cabin tearing off the clothing of the children and half freezing them with cold. The hideous noise of the tempest drowned their melancholy cries and at last they lay quiet and dead.

At the Longstone Lighthouse the morning of the seventh of September broke mistily. The dwellers there were but three—the keeper and his wife and daughter. They were used to raging seas and driving winds, but this night had been one of anxiety. Grace, it is said, had been unable to sleep, and as she dozed toward morning had started up with a wail for help echoing in her ears. She roused her father and taking his field-glass sought the wreck which she felt must be near. The remains of the shattered vessel lying about a mile off met her eye, and dim figures clinging to the broken timbers. As the waters lashed the wreck it seemed as if each wave must sweep the forms into the sea.

The hearts of all three of the lighthouse family sank. What could three do and the billows running mountains? William Darling shrank from attempting any rescue. He had been on other humane enterprises. But this seemed futile. At Grace's earnest plea the boat was launched, her father yielding to her entreaties, which his heart said were right. Grace sprang in—she knew how to handle an oar—and her father followed. She had never assisted in the boat before this wreck of the *Forfarshire*, but other members of the family had been present.

Her mother, Mrs. Darling, had assisted in making the boat ready, but as her husband and daughter pushed off, and the waves washed the rock on which she stood, she cried with tears in her eyes:

"Oh, Grace, if your father is lost, I'll blame you for this morning's work."

Says one who told the story:

"In estimating the dangers which heroic adventurers encounter, one circumstance ought not to be forgotten. Had it been at ebb tide the boat could not have passed between the islands; and Darling and his daughter knew that the tide would be flowing on their return, when their united strength would have been utterly insufficient to pull the boat back to the lighthouse island. Had they not got aid of the survivors in rowing back again, they themselves would have been compelled to remain on the rock beside the wreck until the tide ebbed again."

The frail boat passed over the stormy waters and neared the rock.

It could only have been by the exertion of muscular power as well as determined courage that the father and daughter carried the boat to the rock. And when there a danger, greater even than that which they had encountered in approaching it, arose from the difficulty of steadying the boat and preventing its being destroyed on those sharp ridges by the ever-restless chafing and heaving of the billows.

The father and daughter could see the eager faces turned toward them, and the sight redoubled their efforts in reaching the rock, and in the task of disembarking and drawing the boat up the rock and out of reach of the waves. It was a perilous landing-place. But when the craft was secured the father and Grace approached the half-dead group.

All were safe except the two children. Their mother was seemingly dead, also, and lay clasping the bodies in her arms. But care and attention revived her. A fireman who had lain for three hours on the rock where he had been tossed, had clung to a strong nail spiked in the rock, and though lashed and beaten by the waves, and tortured by bleeding hands, he had not let go.

The rescuers placed the survivors one by one in the boat. But the return journey was even more perilous than that which took them to the wreck, although the sailors aided at the oars. Longstone, however, was at last reached and the sufferers housed in the lighthouse.

They were in safety, but the violence of the sea forbade any attempt to reach the mainland. There were good accommodations at the light. The tower was ingeniously built, and besides a well-furnished sitting-room, in which was a capital collection of books, had three or four comfortable bedrooms. In addition there was an abundance of wholesome, homely fare.

The poor woman who had lost her children was suffering intensely, and to her Grace gave up her bed, sleeping upon a table. A boat's crew from Northumberland, which after some hours came in search of the *Forfarshire*, also had to claim the hospitality of the lighthouse, and for three days were held by the raging seas. Finally, the passage to the mainland was undertaken in safety, and the news reached the keeper's family that the boat first launched had been picked up and its nine passengers rescued. Of the sixty-three who had sailed from Hull five days before, nineteen were alive.

Within a few days search was made for the missing bodies, but almost in vain. The cargo of the steamer, which was of unusual value was wholly lost. The wreck, consisting of the engine, paddle-wheels, anchor, foremast and rigging, remained upon the rock and was visited by thousands.

Report of Grace Darling's heroic deed was soon spread throughout England. It was a simple, humane action and such actions are doing among us all the time. But the courage in facing the elemental rage of the sea, and the helpful sympathy with the unfortunate which it made evident, appealed to the popular heart, and Grace became a people's heroine. Public subscriptions were at once set on foot to express by a splendid gift the universal sense of her deserts. Many smaller tokens also came to her. Among them was a silver medal which read:

Presented by the Glasgow Humane Society to Miss Grace Horsley Darling, in admiration of her dauntless and heroic conduct in saving (along with her father) the lives of nine persons from the wreck of the *Forfarshire* steamer, 7th September, 1838.

So great was popular report and admiration for the heroine that the manager of a theatre broached to her the plan of representing the rescue, in part at least, upon his stage, and offered her a considerable sum for sitting in the boat for the audience to view. Her portrait was taken and sold everywhere. She was generally flattered and caressed.

It was now that we find the true balance and strength in Grace's character. The testimonials she received with quiet pleasure. But she preferred to remain upon the solitary island under the light, and aid her mother in her simple household work.

She was glad to have saved lives at the risk of her own, she said, and would most willingly do it again if opportunity should occur. But she could not feel that she had done anything great, and certainly she did not wish for the praise that had been bestowed upon her. As for going to the theatre to receive the plaudits of a curious crowd, that was the last thing she desired.

Of Grace at this time the pleasing English writer, William Howitt, gives this account. He paid a visit to Longstone and met the heroine:

"When I went she was not visible, and I was afraid I should not see her, as her father said she very much disliked meeting strangers that she thought came to stare at her; but when the old man and I had had a little conversation he went up to her room, and soon came down with a smile, saying that she would be with us soon. So when we had been up to the top lighthouse, and had seen its machinery, and taken a good look-out at the distant shore, and Darling had pointed out the spot of the wreck, and the way they took the people off, we went down and found Grace sitting at her sewing, very neatly but very simply dressed in a plain sort of striped print gown, with her watch-seal just seen at her side and her hair neatly braided—just, in fact, as such girls are dressed, only not quite so smart as they often are. She rose, very modestly, and with a pleasant smile said: 'How do you do, sir?'

"Her figure is by no means striking—quite the contrary; but her face it full of sense, modesty and genuine goodness; and that is just the character she bears. Her prudence delights one. We are charmed that she should so well have supported the brilliancy of her humane deeds. It is confirmative of the notion that such actions must spring from genuine heart and mind."

She had the sweetest smile, continued Mr. Howitt, that he had ever seen in a person of her station and appearance. "You see that she is a thoroughly good creature, and that under her modest exterior lies a spirit capable of the most exalted devotion, a devotion so entire that daring is not so much a quality of her nature, as that the most perfect sympathy with suffering or endangered humanity swallows up and annihilates everything like fear or self-consideration, puts out, in fact, every sentiment but itself."

As we read above Grace was slight of frame, and not markedly robust. Barely three years after the wreck at which her pity and heroism had won her world-wide fame, she showed evidences of decline. Toward the close of 1841 she was taken from Longstone and placed under the care of a doctor in Bamborough. Not gaining in strength she begged to be moved to Wooler, a small market town on the border of Northumberland, where the scenery is of the Cheviot Hills—of sunny heights and wooded glens. But even here the clear bracing air had little help for her illness, and after meeting her father and considering her failing strength, with his advice she returned to Bamborough. Her eldest sister nursed her with devotion, but it was evident her life was fading.

Throughout her illness she never murmured and never complained, we are are told, and shortly before her death she expressed a wish to see as many of her relations as the peculiar nature of their employment would admit, and with surprising fortitude and self-command she delivered to each one of them some token of remembrance. This done she calmly awaited the approach of death; and finally, on October 20, 1842, resigned her spirit without a murmur.

Two stones have been raised to her memory, one in the Bamborough churchyard, her figure lying at length; and another in the chapel of St. Cuthbert, on one of the Farne Islands, and bearing this memorial:

TO THE MEMORY OF
Grace Horsley Darling
A NATIVE OF BAMBOROUGH AND AN INHABITANT
OF THESE ISLANDS
WHO DIED OCTOBER 20TH, 1842,
AGED 26 YEARS.

But the best memorial of a heroine is the inspiration her example offers to her own generation and those that succeed her, the love her deeds engender in other hearts, the enlarging and uplifting of our kind through her endeavour. And so it is that the heroine of Farne Islands has become a lovely memory to us, and to those who shall come after us.

XII

SISTER DORA

Dorothy Wyndlow Pattison was born on January 15th, 1832. She was the youngest daughter, and the youngest child but one, of the Rev. Mark Pattison, who was for many years Rector of Hauxwell, near Richmond, in Yorkshire. She inherited from her father, who was of a Devonshire family, that finely proportioned and graceful figure which she always maintained; and from her mother, who was the daughter of a banker in Richmond, those lovely features which drew forth the admiration of everyone who had the pleasure of knowing her.

Her father was a good and sincere man. He was thoroughly upright and strict.

Dora and her sister, like a thousand other country parsons' daughters, were of the utmost use in their father's Yorkshire parish. A French gentleman who had lived a while in England and in the country, said to me one day:

"Your young ladies astound me. They are angels of mercy. They wear no distinguishing habit; one does not see their wings, yet they fly everywhere, and everywhere bring grace and love and peace—in my country such a thing would be impossible."

These Pattison girls were for ever saving their pocket money to give it away, and they made it a rule to mend and remake their old frocks, so as not to have to buy new ones out of their allowance for clothes, so as to have more to give. Even their dinners they would reserve for poor people, and content themselves with bread and cheese. "Giving to others instead of spending on themselves seems to have been the rule and delight of their lives."

A pretty story is told of Dorothy at this time. A schoolboy in the village, who was especially attached to her, fell ill of rheumatic fever. The boy's one longing was to see "Miss Dora" again, but she was abroad on the Continent. As he grew worse and worse, he constantly prayed that he might live long enough to see her. On the day on which she was expected, he sat up on his pillows intently listening, and at last, long before anyone else could hear a sound of wheels, he exclaimed: "There she is!" and sank back. She went to him at once, and nursed him till he died.

Her beauty was very great: large brilliant, brown eyes, full red lips, a firm chin and a finely cut profile; her hair dark, and slightly curling, waved all over her head; and the remarkable beauty and delicacy of her colouring and complexion, added to the liveliness of her expression, made her a fascinating creature to behold. Her father always called her "Little Sunshine."

But the most remarkable feature about her was to be found in her inner being. A will, which no earthly power could subdue, enabled her to accomplish an almost superhuman work; yet at times it was to her a faculty that brought her into difficulties. She was twenty-nine before she was able to find real scope for her energies, and then she took a bold step—answered an advertisement from a clergyman for a lady to take the village school. Her mother had died in 1861, and she considered herself free from duties that bound her to her home. Her father did not relish the step she took, but acquiesced. She went to Woolston, and remained there three years, during which time she won the hearts, not of the children only, but of their parents as well. She had to live alone in a cottage, and do everything for her self; but the people never for a moment doubted she was a real lady, and always treated her with great respect.

Not thinking a little village school sufficient field for her energies, she resolved to join a nursing sisterhood at Redcar, in Yorkshire. The life was not quite suited to her strong will, but it did her good. She there learned how to make beds and to cook. At first she literally sat down and cried when the beds which she had just put in order were all pulled to pieces by some superior authority, who did not approve of the method in which they were made. But it was a useful lesson for her after life in a hospital. She was there till the early part of 1865, and then was sent to Walsall to help at a small cottage hospital, which had already been established for more than a year.

Walsall, though not in the "Black Country," is in a busy manufacturing district, chiefly of iron. At the time when Sister Dora went there it contained a population of 35,000 inhabitants. It is now connected with Birmingham by almost continuous houses and pits and furnaces.

As fresh coal and iron pits were being opened in the district around Walsall, accidents became more frequent, and it was found impracticable to send those injured to Birmingham, which was seven miles distant; Accordingly, in 1863, the Town Council invited the Redcar Society to start a hospital there. When the Sister who had begun the work fell ill, Sister Dora was sent in her place, and almost directly caught small-pox from the outpatients. She was very ill, and even in her delirium showed the bent of her mind by ripping her sheets into strips to serve as bandages.

When the cottage hospital—which was the second of its kind in England—was opened, the system of voluntary nursing was unknown; the only voluntary nurses heard of then being those who had gone out to the Crimea with Miss Florence Nightingale. Therefore a good deal of misunderstanding was the result; but in the course of time people began to judge the institution by its results. But Sister Dora, by her frank, open manner, disarmed suspicion, while the sublime eloquence of noble deeds silenced tongues, and won for the hospital the confidence of the public, and for herself the admiration and affection of the people.

In 1866 she had a serious illness, brought on by exposure to wet and cold. She would come home from dressing wounds in the cottages, wet through and hot with hurrying along the streets, to find a crowd of outpatients awaiting her return at the hospital, and she would attend to them in total disregard of herself, and allow her wet clothes to dry on her.

This neglect occurred once too often; a chill settled on her, and for three weeks she was dangerously ill. Then it was that the people of Walsall began to realise what she was, and the door of the hospital was besieged by poor people come to inquire how their "Sister Dora" was.

The hospital had moved men of every shade of politics, and every form of religious belief, to the work, and there have been passages in its history not pleasant to remember, but not one of these in the remotest degree involved Sister Dora. On the contrary, her presence and counsel always brought light and peace, and lifted every question into a higher sphere. "Ask Sister Dora," it used to be said. "Had we not better send for Sister Dora" some member would exclaim out of the fog of contention. Thereupon she would appear; and many well remember how calmly self-possessed, and clear-sighted she would stand—never sit down. Indeed, there were those who worked with her fifteen years who never saw her seated; she would stand, usually with her hand on the back of the chair which had been placed for her, every eye directed to her; nor was it ever many moments before she had grasped the whole question, and given her opinion just as clearly and simply and straight to the purpose as any opinion given to the sufferers in the wards. Nor was she ever wrong; nor did she ever fail of her purpose with the committee. No committeemen ever questioned or differed from Sister Dora, yet in her was the charm of unconsciousness of power or superiority and the impression left was of there being no feeling of pleasure in her, other than the triumph of the right.

In 1867 the cottage hospital had to be abandoned, as erysipelas broke out and would not be expelled. The wards were evidently impregnated with malignant germs to such an extent that the committee resolved to build a new hospital in a better situation.

Sister Dora's work became more engrossing when this larger field was opened for it; the men's beds were constantly full, and even the women's ward was hardly ever entirely empty.

Just at this period an epidemic of small-pox broke out in Walsall, and all the energies of Sister Dora were called into play. She visited the cottages where the patients lay, and nursed them or saw to their being supplied with what they needed; whilst at the same time carrying on her usual work at the hospital.

One night she was sent for by a poor man who was dying of what she called "black-pox," a violent form of small-pox. She went at once, and found him in the last extremity. All his relations had fled, and a neighbour alone was with him. When Sister Dora found that only one small piece of candle was left in the house, she gave the woman some money, begging her to go and buy some means of light whilst she stayed with the man. She sat on by his bed, but the woman, who had probably spent the money at the public house, never returned; and after some little while the dying man raised himself up in bed with a last effort, saying, "Sister, kiss me before I die." She took him, all covered as he was with the loathsome disease, into her arms and kissed him, the candle going out almost as she did so, leaving them in total darkness. He implored her not to leave him while he lived, although he might have known she would never do that. So she sat through the night, till the early dawn breaking in revealed that the man was dead.

When the bell at the head of her bed rang at night she rose at once, saying to herself, "The Master is come, and calleth for thee!" Indeed, she loved to think that she was ministering to her Lord in the person of His poor and sick.

Here is a letter from a former patient in the hospital, from which only a short extract can be made:

"I had not been there above a week when Sister Dora found me a little bell, as there was not one to my bed, and she said, 'Enoch, you must ring this bell when you want sister.' This little bell did not have much rest, for whenever I heard her step or the tinkle of her keys in the hall I used to ring my bell, and she would call out, 'I'm coming, Enoch,' which she did, and would say, 'What do you want?' I often used to say, 'I don't know, Sister,' not really knowing what I did want. She'd say, 'Do you want your pillows shaken up, or do you want moving a little?' which she'd do, whatever it was, and say, 'Do you feel quite cosey now?' 'Yes, Sister.' Then she would start to go into the other ward, but very often before she could get through the door I'd call her back and say my pillow wasn't quite right, or that my leg wanted moving a little. She would come and do it, whatever it was, and say, 'Will that do?' 'Yes, Sister.' Then she'd go about her work, but at the very next sound of her step my bell would ring, and so often as my bell rang Sister would come; and some of the other patients would often remark that I should wear that little bell out or Sister, and she'd say, 'Never mind, for I like to hear it, and it's never too often.' And it rang so often that I've heard Sister say that she often dreamt she heard my little bell and started up in a hurry to find it was a dream."

Sister Dora said once to a friend, who was engaging a servant for the hospital:

"Tell her this is not an ordinary house, or even a hospital. I want her to understand that all who serve here, in whatever capacity, ought to have one rule, *love for God*, and then, I need not say, love for their work."

She spoke often and with intense earnestness, on the duty, the necessity, of prayer. It was literally true that she never touched a wound without raising her heart to God and entreating him to bless the means employed. As years glided away, she became able almost to fulfil the Apostle's command: "Pray without ceasing." And her prayers were animated by the most intense faith—an absolutely unshaken conviction of their efficacy. It may truly be said that those who pray become increasingly more sure of the value of prayer. They find that, whatever men may say about the reign of law and the order of nature, earnest prayer does bring an answer, often in a marvellous manner. The praying man or woman is never shaken in his or her trust in the efficacy of prayer. She firmly held to the supernatural power, put into the hands of men by means of the weapon of prayer; and the practical faithlessness in this respect of the world at large was an ever-increasing source of surprise and distress to her.

Since her death, in commemoration of her labours at Walsall, a very beautiful statue has been there erected to her, and on the pedestal are bas-reliefs representing incidents in her life there. One of these illustrates a terrible explosion that took place in the Birchett's Iron Works, on Friday, October 15, 1875, whereby eleven men were so severely burnt that only two survived. All the others died after their admission into the hospital. It came about thus: The men were at work when water escaped from the "twyer" and fell upon the molten iron in the furnace and was at once resolved into steam that blew out the front of the furnace, and also the molten iron, which fell upon the men. Some suffered frightful agonies, but the shock to the nervous systems of others had stupefied them. The sight and the smell were terrible. Ladies who volunteered their help could not endure it, and were forced to withdraw, some not getting beyond the door of the ward. But Sister Dora was with the patients incessantly till they died, giving them water, bandaging their wounds, or cutting away the sodden clothes that adhered to the burnt flesh. Some lingered on for ten days, but in all this time she never deserted the fetid atmosphere of the ward, never went to bed.

She had so much to do with burns that she became specially skilful in treating them. Children terribly burnt or scalded were constantly brought to the hospital; often men came scalded from a boiler, or by molten metal. She dressed their wounds herself, but, if possible, always sent the patients to be tended at home, where she would visit them and regularly dress their wounds, rather than have the wards tainted by the effluvium from the burns. Her treatment of burnt children merits quotation.

"If a large surface of the body was burnt, or if the child seemed beside itself with terror, she did not touch the wounds themselves, but only carefully excluded the air from them by means of cotton wool and blankets wrapped around the body. She put hot bottles and flannel to the feet, and, if necessary, ice to the head. Then she gave her attention to soothing and consoling the shocked nerves—a state which she considered to be often a more immediate source of danger to the life of the child than the actual injuries. She fed it with milk and brandy, unless it violently refused food, when she would let it alone until it came round, saying that force, or anything which involved even a slight further shock to the system, was worse than useless. Sometimes, of course, the fatal sleep of exhaustion, from which there was no awakening, would follow; but more often than not food was successfully administered, and after a few hours, Sister Dora, having gained the child's confidence, could dress the wounds without fear of exciting the frantic terror which would have been the result of touching them at first."

Children Sister Dora dearly loved; her heart went out to them with infinite tenderness, and she was even known to sleep with a burnt baby on each arm. What that means only those know who have had experience of the sickening smell arising from burns.

Once a little girl of nine was brought into the hospital so badly burnt that it was obvious she had not many hours to live. Sister Dora sat by her bed talking to her of Jesus Christ and His love for little children, and of the blessed home into which he would receive them. The child died peacefully, and her last words were: "Sister, when you come to heaven, I'll meet you at the gates with a bunch of flowers."

One of the most heroic of her many heroic acts was taking charge of the small-pox hospital when a second epidemic broke out.

Mr. S. Welsh says: "In the spring of 1875 there was a second visitation of the disease, and fears were entertained that the results would be as bad as during the former visitation. One morning Sister Dora came to me and said, 'Do you know, I have an idea that if some one could be got to go to the epidemic hospital in whom the people have confidence, they would send their friends to be nursed, the patients would be isolated, and the disease stamped out.'" This was because a prejudice was entertained against the new small-pox hospital, and those who had sick concealed the fact rather than send them to it. "I said," continues Mr. Welsh, "'I have long been of the opinion you have just expressed; but where are we to get a lady, in whom the people would have confidence, to undertake the duty?'

"Her prompt reply was, 'I will go.'

"I confess the sudden announcement of her determination rather took me by surprise, for I had no expectation of it, and not the least remote idea that she intended to go. 'But,' I said, 'who will take charge of the hospital if you go there?'

"'Oh,' she replied, 'I can get plenty of ladies to come there, but none will go to the epidemic. And', she added, by way of reconciling me to her view, 'it will only be for a short time.'

"'But what if you were to take the disease and die?' I inquired.

"'Then,' she added, in her cheery way, 'I shall have died in the path of duty, and, you know, I could not die better.'

"I knew it was no use pointing out at length the risk she ran, for where it was a case of saving others, *self* with her was no consideration. I tried to dissuade her on other grounds.... A few days later I was in company with the doctor of the hospital, who was also medical officer of health, and who, as such, had charge of the epidemic hospital, near to which we were at the time. He said, 'Do you know where Sister Dora is?' 'At the hospital I suppose,' was my reply. 'No,' he rejoined, 'she is over there!' pointing to the epidemic hospital....

"The people as soon as they knew Sister Dora was in charge, had no misgiving about sending their relatives to be nursed, and the result was as she had predicted; the cases were brought in as soon as it was discovered that patients had the disease, and the epidemic was speedily stamped out."

She had, however, a hard time of it there, as she lacked assistants. Two women were sent from the work-house, but they proved of little use. The porter, an old soldier, was attentive and kind in his way, but he always went out "on a spree" on Saturday nights, and did not return till late on Sunday evening. When the work-house women failed her she was sometimes alone with her patients, and these occasionally in the delirium of small-pox.

It was not till the middle of August, 1875, that the last small-pox patient departed from the hospital, and she was able to return to her original work.

One of the bas-reliefs on her monument represents Sister Dora consoling the afflicted and the scene depicted refers to a dreadful colliery accident that occurred on March 14, 1872, at

Pelsall, a village rather over three miles from Walsall, by which twenty-two men were entombed, and all perished. For several days hopes were entertained that some of the men would be got out alive; and blankets in which to wrap them, and restoratives, were provided, and Sister Dora was sent for to attend the men when brought to "bank." The following extract, from an article by a special correspondent in a newspaper, dated Dec 10, 1872, will give some idea of Sister Dora's connection with the event:

Out of doors the scene is weird and awful, and impresses the mind with a peculiar gloom; for the intensity of the darkness is heightened by the shades created by the artificial lights. Every object, the most minute, stands out in bold relief against the inky darkness which surrounds the landscape. On the crest of the mound or pit-bank, the policemen, like sentinels, are walking their rounds. The wind is howling and whistling through the trees which form a background to the pit-bank, and the rain is coming hissing down in sheets. In a hovel close to the pit shaft sit the bereaved and disconsolate mourners, hoping against hope, and watching for those who will never return. There, too, are the swarthy sons of toil who have just returned from their fruitless search in the mine for the dear missing ones, and are resting while their saturated clothes are drying.

But another form glides softly from that hovel; and amid the pelting rain, and over the rough pit-bank, and through miry clay—now ankle deep—takes her course to the dwellings of the mourners, for some, spent with watching, have been induced to return to their homes. As she plods her way amid pieces of timber, upturned wagons and fragments of broken machinery, which are scattered about in great confusion, a "wee, wee bairn" creeps gently to her side, and grasping her hand and looking wistfully into her face, which is radiant with kindness and affection, says, "Oh, Sister, do see to my father when they bring him up the pit." Poor child! Never again would he know a father's love, or share a father's care. She smiled, and that smile seemed to lighten the child's load of grief, and her promise to see to his father appeared to impart consolation to his heavy, despairing heart.

On she glides, with a kind word or a sympathetic expression to all. One woman, after listening to her comforting words, burst into tears—the fountains of sorrow so long pent up seemed to have found vent. "Let her weep," said a relative of the unfortunate woman; "it is the first tear she has shed since the accident has occurred, and it will do her good to cry." But who is the good Samaritan? She is the sister who for seven years has had the management of the nursing department in the cottage hospital at Walsall.

This is written in too much of the "special correspondent" style to be pleasant; nevertheless it describes what actually took place.

Mr. Samuel Welsh says: "I remember one evening I was in the hospital when a poor man who had been dreadfully crushed in a pit was brought in. One of his legs was so fearfully injured that it was thought it would be necessary to amputate it. After examining the patient, the doctor came to me in the committee-room—one door of which opened into the passage leading to the wards and another into the hall in the domestic portion of the building. After telling me about the patient who had just been brought in, he said, 'Do you know Sister Dora is very ill? So ill,' he continued, 'that I question if she will pull through this time.' I naturally inquired what she was suffering from, and in reply the doctor said, 'She will not take care of herself, and is suffering from blood-poison.' He left me, and I was just trying to solve the problem—'What shall be done? or how shall her place be supplied if she be taken from us by death?' when I saw a spectral-like figure gliding gently and almost noiselessly through the room from the domestic entrance to the door leading to the wards. The figure was rather indistinct, for it was nearly dark; and as I gazed at the receding form, I said, 'Sister, is it you?' 'Whist!' she said, and glided through the doorway into the wards. In a short time she returned, and I said to her, 'Sister, the doctor has just been telling me how ill you are—how is it you are here?' 'Ah!' replied, she 'it is true I am very ill; but I heard the surgeons talking about amputating that poor fellow's limb, and I wanted to see whether or not there was a possibility of saving it, and I believe there is; and, knowing that, I shall rest better.' So saying, she glided as noiselessly out of the room as when she entered.

"On her recovery—which was retarded by her neglecting herself to attend to others—she called me one day to the hall-door of the hospital, and asked me if I thought it was going to rain. I told her I did not think it would rain for some hours. She then told me to go and order a cab to be ready at the hospital in half an hour. I tried to persuade her not to venture out so soon; but it was no use—she went; and many a time I wondered where she went to.

"About six months afterward I happened to be at a railway station, and saw a pointsman who had been in our hospital with an injured foot, but who, as his friends wished to have him at home, had left before his foot was cured. I inquired how his foot was. He replied that had it not been for Sister Dora he would have lost his foot, if not his life. I said, 'How did she save your foot when you were not in the hospital, and she was ill at the time you left the hospital?' 'Well,' he replied, 'you know my foot was far from well when I left the hospital; there was no one at our house who could see to it properly, and it took bad ways, and one evening I was in awful pain. Oh, how I did wish for Sister Dora to come and dress it! I felt sure she could give me relief, but I had been told she was very ill, so I had no hope that my earnest desire would be realised; but while I was thinking and wishing, the bedroom door was gently opened, and a figure just like Sister Dora glided so softly into the room that I could not hear her, but oh! she was so pale that I began to think it must be her spirit but when she folded the bedclothes from off my foot, I knew it was she. She dressed my foot, and from that hour it began to improve.'

"A few days after this interview with the pointsman I was talking to Sister Dora, and said: 'By the bye, Sister, I have found out where you went with the cab that day.' She replied with a merry twinkle in her eye, 'What a long time you have been finding it out!'"

Her old patients ever remembered her with gratitude. A man called Chell, an engine-stoker, was twice in the hospital under her care, first with a dislocated ankle, severely cut; the second time with a leg crushed to pieces in a railway accident. It was amputated. According to his own account he remembered nothing of the operation, except that Sister Dora was there, and that, "When I come to after the chloroform, she was on her knees by my side with her arm supporting my head, and she was repeating:

"'They climbed the steep ascent of heaven, Through peril, toil and pain: O God, to us may grace be given To follow in their train.'

And all through the pain and trouble that I had afterward, I never forgot Sister's voice saying those words." When she was in the small-pox hospital, avoided by most, this man never failed to stump away to it to see her and inquire how she was getting on.

There were, as she herself recognised, faults in the character of Sister Dora; and yet, without these faults, problematical as it may seem, it is doubtful whether she could have achieved all she did.

One who knew her long and intimately writes to me "A majestic character, brimming over with sympathy, but, for lack of self-discipline, this sympathy was impulsive and gushing. Her glorious nature, physical and mental, was marred by undisciplined impulse. Her nature found its congenial outlet in devoted works of mercy and love to her fellow creatures. How far she would have done the same under authority, I fear is a little doubtful."

Miss Twigg, who knew her well, writes me: "She was a lovable woman, so bright and winsome. She used to come into our rather dull and sad home (our mother died when we were quite children) after evening service. She would nurse one of us, big as we were then, and the others would gather round her, while she would tell us stories of her hospital life.... She was a *real* woman."

There is one point in Sister Dora's life to which sufficient attention has not been paid by her biographers. It is one which the busy workers of the present day think of too little—namely, the writing of bright, helpful letters to any friend who is sick or in trouble. Somehow or other she always found time for that, wrote one who knew her well, and who contributes the following, written to a young girl who was at the time in a spinal hospital, and who was almost a stranger to her:

My dear Miss J.—I was so glad to hear from you, though I fear it must be a trouble for you to write. I *do* hope that you will really have benefited by the treatment and rest. I am so glad that the doctor is good to his "children." Such little attentions when you are sick help to alleviate wonderfully. I wish I could come and take a peep at you. Did Mrs. N. tell you that she had sent us five pounds for our seaside expedition? Was it not good of her? Oh! we shall have such a jolly time. To see all those poor creatures drink in the sea-breezes! We have had a very busy week of accidents and operations. It has been a regular storm.[1] My dear, it is in such times as you are now having that the voice of Jesus Christ can be best heard, "Come into a desert place awhile." Know you surely that it is God's visitation. Take home that thought, realise it: God *visiting you.* Elizabeth was astonished that the Mother of her Lord should visit her. We can have our Emmanuel. I can look back on my sicknesses as the best times of my life. Don't fret about the future. He carrieth our sicknesses and healeth our infirmities. You know infirmity means weakness after sickness. Think of the cheering lines of our hymn: "His touch has still its ancient power." When I arose up from my sick bed they told me I should never be able to enter a hospital or do work again. I was fretting over this when a good friend came to me, and told me only to take a day's burden and not look forward, and it was such a help. I got up every day feeling sure I should have strength and grace for the day's trial. May it be said

---

[1] A Yorkshire expression for heavy work.

of you, dear, "They took knowledge of her that she had been with Jesus." May He reveal Himself in all His beauty is the prayer of

Your sincere friend,
Sister Dora.

It does not truly represent Sister Dora to dwell on her outer life, and not look as well into that which is within, as it was the very mainspring of all her actions, as it, in fact, made her what she was.

The same writer to the *Guardian* gives some sentences from other letters: "Take your cross day by day, dearie, and with Jesus Christ bearing the other end it will not be *too* heavy." "If we could find Jesus, it must be on a mountain, not in the plains or smooth places." "He went up into a mountain and taught them, saying," etc. "It is only on a mountain side that we shall see the cross. It was only after Zacchæus had *climbed* the tree he could see Jesus. I have been thinking much of this lately. It is not in the smooth places we shall see Jesus, it is in the rough, in the storm, or by the sick couch." "A Christian is one whose object is Christ." "I am rejoiced that you are enjoying Faber's hymns; they always *warm* me up. Oh, my dear, is it not sad that we prefer to live in the shade when we might have the glorious sunshine?"

It was during the winter of 1876-77 that Sister Dora felt the first approach of the terrible disease that was to cause her death, and then it was rather by diminution of strength than by actual pain. She consulted a doctor in Birmingham, in whom she placed confidence, and he told her the plain truth, that her days in this world were numbered. She exacted from him a pledge of secrecy, and then went on with her work as hitherto.

"She was suddenly brought, as it were, face to face with death—distant, perhaps, but inevitable; she, who was full of such exuberant life and spirit that the very word 'death' seemed a contradiction when applied to her. Even her doctor, as he looked at her blooming appearance, and measured with his eye her finely made form, was almost inclined to believe the evidence of his outward senses against his sober judgment.... She could not endure pity. She, to whom everybody had learnt instinctively to turn for help and consolation, on whom others leant for support, must she now come down to ask of them sympathy and comfort? The pride of life was still surging up in her, that pride which had made her glory in her physical strength for its own sake, as well as for its manifold uses in the service of her Master. True, she had been long living two lives inseparably blended: the outward life of hard, unceasing toil; the inner, a constant communion with the unseen world, the existence of which she realised to an extent which not even those who saw the most of her could appreciate. To all the poor, ignorant beings whose souls she tried to reach by means of their maimed bodies, she was, indeed, the personification of all that they could conceive as lovable, holy and merciful in the Saviour. At the same time she judged her own self with strict impartiality. She knew her own faults, her unbending will—her pride and glory in her work seemed to her even a fault; and, in place of looking on herself as perfect she was bowed down with a sense of her own short-comings. At the same time—with death before her, she hungered for more work for her Master. His words were continually on her lips: 'I must work the works of Him that sent me while it is day; the night cometh when no man can work.'"

At last, in the month of August, 1878, typhoid fever having broken out in the temporary hospital, it was found necessary to close it, and hasten on the work of the construction of another. This gave her an opportunity for a holiday and a complete change. She went to the Isle of Man, to London, and to Paris.

But the disorder was making rapid strides, and was causing her intense suffering, and she craved to be back at Walsall. She got as far as Birmingham, and was then in such a critical state that it was feared she would die. But her earnest entreaty was to be taken to Walsall. "Let me die," she pleaded, "among my own people."

Mr. Welsh says: "On calling at the Queen's Hotel, Birmingham (where she was lying ill), I was told the doctor of the hospital (Dr. Maclachlan) was with her, and thinking they were probably arranging matters connected with the hospital, I did not go to her room, but proceeded to the train. I had scarcely got seated when the doctor called me out, and we entered a compartment where we were alone. He asked me when it was intended to open the hospital. I replied, 'On the 4th of November.' 'Then,' he said, 'that will just be about the same time Sister Dora will die.'

"The announcement was to me a shock of no ordinary kind, for I had not heard of her being ill, and no one could have imagined, from the cheerful tone of a letter I had received from her a week or so before, that there was anything the matter with her. Not being able to fully realise the true state of affairs, I asked him if he were jesting. He replied he was not, and that he thought it best to let me know at once, so that arrangements might be made for getting someone to take her place when the hospital was opened. I said, 'I suppose she is going to Yorkshire?' 'No,' he replied, 'and that is another thing I wish to speak to you about. She wishes to die in Walsall, and she must be removed immediately.'

"On Sunday (the day following) I saw the chairman and vice-chairman of the hospital. On Sunday evening I returned with Dr. Maclachlan to the Queen's Hotel, where he found his patient very weak. On Monday morning a house was taken, and the furniture she had in her rooms at the hospital removed to it. Her old servant who had gone to The Potteries, was telegraphed for, and arrived in a few hours, and by midday the house was ready for her reception. My daughter, knowing Sister Dora's fondness for flowers, had procured and placed on the table in the parlour a very choice bouquet; and when all was ready Dr. Maclachlan drove over to Birmingham, and brought her to Walsall in his private carriage.

"The disease was now making steady progress, and it was evident that every day she was becoming weaker; but she never lost her cheerfulness, and anyone to have seen her might have thought she was only suffering from some slight ailment, instead of an incurable and painful disease."

"A few hours before her death," writes Mr. S. Welsh "she called me to her bedside and said, 'I want you to promise that you will not, when I am gone, write anything about me; *quietly I came among you and, quietly I wish to go away.*'" And this desire of hers would have been faithfully complied with had not misrepresentations fired the gentleman to whom the request was made to take up his pen, not in defence of her, but in the correction of statements that affected certain persons who were alive.

In her last sickness when she found her end approaching, she insisted on every one leaving the room—it was her wish to die alone. And as she persisted, so was it, only one nurse standing by the door held ajar, and watching till she knew by the change of attitude, and a certain fixed look in the countenance, that Sister Dora had entered into her rest.[2]

"It was Christmas Eve when she passed away, and a dense fog, like a funeral pall, hung over the town and obscured every object a few feet from the ground. Under this strange canopy the market was being held, and people were busy buying and selling, and making preparations for the great Christmas festival on the following day; but when the deep boom of the passing bell announced the melancholy intelligence that Sister Dora had entered into her rest, a thrill of horror ran through the people, who, with blanched cheeks and bated breath, whispered, 'Can it be true?' Although for seven weeks the process of dissolution had been going on before their eyes, they could not realise the fact that she whom they loved and revered was no more."

The funeral took place on Saturday, the 28th of December. "The day was dark and dismal, the streets, covered with slush and

---

[2] This has been denied. Her old and devoted servant said: "Do you think I would let my darling die alone?" But it appears to me that Sister Dora's desire was one to be expected in such a spiritual nature; and in the statement above given it is not said that she was actually left in solitude.

sludge caused by the melted snow, were thronged with spectators.... There was general mourning in the town; and although it was market day nearly every shop was closed during the time of the funeral, and all the blinds along the route of the procession were drawn.... On reaching the cemetery it was found that four other funerals had arrived from the workhouse; and as these coffins had been taken into the chapel there was no room for Sister Dora's, which had, consequently, to be placed in the porch. This was as Sister Dora would have wished, had she had the ordering of the arrangements, for she always gave preference to the poor, to whom she was attached in life, and from whom she would not have desired to be separated in death."

True to her thought of others, in the midst of her last sufferings, she had made arrangements for a Christmas dinner to be given to a number of her old patients, in accordance with a custom of hers in previous years; but on this occasion the festive proceedings were shorn of their gladness. All thought of her who in her pain and on her deathbed had thought of them. Every one tried, but ineffectually, to cheer and comfort the other, but the task was hopeless. One young lady, after the meal, and while the Christmas tree was being lighted commenced singing the pretty little piece, "Far Away," but when she came to the words:

Some are gone from us forever Longer here they could not stay,

she burst into tears; and the women present sobbed, and tears were seen stealing down the cheeks of bearded men.

The Walsall writer of "A Review" concludes his paper thus:

She is no idol to us, but we worship her memory as the most saintly thing that was ever given us. Her name is immortalised, both by her own surpassing goodness, and by the love of a whole people for her—a love that will survive through generations, and give a magic and a music to those simple words, "Sister Dora," long after we shall have passed away. There was little we could ever do—there was nothing she would let us do—to relieve the self-imposed rigours of her life; but we love her in all sincerity, and now in our helplessness we find a serene joy in the knowledge that to her, as surely as to any human soul, will be spoken the divine words: "Inasmuch as ye have done it unto the least of these my brethren, ye have done it unto Me."

In Sister Dora, surely we have the highest type of the Christian life, the inner and hidden life of the soul, the life that is hid in God, combined with that outer life devoted to the doing of good to suffering and needy humanity. In the cloistered nun we see only the first, and that tends to become self-centred and morbid; it is redeemed from this vice by an active life of self-sacrifice.

I cannot do better than, in conclusion, quote from the last letter ever penned by Sister Dora:

"It is 2.30 A.M., and I cannot sleep, so I am going to write to you. I was anything but 'forbearing,' dear; I was overbearing, and I am truly sorry for it now. I look back on my life and see 'nothing but leaves.' Oh, my darling, let me speak to you from my deathbed, and say, watch in all you do that you have a single aim—*God's* honour and glory. 'I came not to work my own work, but the works of Him that sent me.' Look upon working as a privilege. Do not look upon nursing in the way they do so much nowadays, as an art or science, but as work done for Christ. As you touch each patient, think it is Christ Himself, and then virtue will come out of the touch to yourself. I have felt that myself, when I have had a particularly loathsome patient. Be full of the Glad Tidings, and you will tell others. You cannot give what you have not got."

XIII

FLORENCE NIGHTINGALE

Day unto day her dainty hands Make Life's soiled temples clean; And there's a wake of glory where Her spirit pure hath been. At midnight through the shadow-land Her living face doth gleam; The dying kiss her shadow, and The dead smile in their dream. —*Gerald Massey.*

Some years ago, when the celebrated Florence Nightingale was a little girl, living at her father's home, a large, old Elizabethan house, with great woods about it, in Hampshire, there was one thing that struck everybody who knew her. It was that she seemed to be always thinking what she could do to please or help anyone who needed either help or comfort. She was very fond, too, of animals, and she was so gentle in her way, that even the shyest of them would come quite close to her, and pick up whatever she flung down for them to eat.

There was, in the garden behind the house, a long walk with trees on each side, the abode of many squirrels, and when Florence came down the walk, dropping nuts as she went along, the squirrels would run down the trunks of their trees, and, hardly waiting until she passed by, would pick up the prize and dart away, with their little bushy tails curled over their backs, and their black eyes looking about as if terrified at the least noise, though they did not seem to be afraid of Florence.

Then there was an old gray pony named Peggy, past work, living in a paddock, with nothing to do all day long but to amuse herself. Whenever Florence appeared at the gate, Peggy would come trotting up and put her nose into the dress pocket of her little mistress, and pick it of the apple or the roll of bread that she knew she would always find there, for this was a trick Florence had taught the pony. Florence was fond of riding, and her father's old friend, the clergyman of the parish, used often to come and take her for a ride with him when he went to the farm cottages at a distance.

As he had studied medicine when a young man, he was able to tell the people what would do them good when they were ill or had met with an accident. Little Florence took great delight in helping to nurse those who were ill; and whenever she went on these long rides, she had a small basket fastened to her saddle, filled with something nice which she saved from her breakfast or dinner, or carried for her mother.

There lived in one of two or three solitary cottages in the wood an old shepherd of her father's, named Roger, who had a favourite sheep-dog called Cap. Roger had neither wife nor child, and Cap lived with him and kept him company at night after he had penned his flock. Cap was a very sensible dog; indeed people used to say he could do everything but speak. He kept the sheep in wonderfully good order, and thus saved his master a great deal of trouble. One day as Florence and her old friend were out for a ride, they came to a field where they found the shepherd giving his sheep their night feed; but he was without the dog, and the sheep knew it, for they were scampering in every direction. Florence and her friend noticed that the old shepherd looked very sad, and they stopped to ask what was the matter, and what had become of his dog.

"Oh," said Roger, "Cap will never be of any more use to me; I'll have to hang him, poor fellow, as soon as I go home to-night."

"Hang him!" said Florence. "Oh, Roger, how wicked of you! What has dear old Cap done?"

"He has done nothing," replied Roger; "but he will never be of any more use to me, and I cannot afford to keep him for nothing; one of the mischievous school boys throwed a stone at him yesterday and broke one of his legs." And the old shepherd's eyes filled with tears, which he wiped away with his shirt-sleeve, then he drove his spade deep in the ground to hide what he felt, for he did not like to be seen crying.

"Poor Cap," he sighed, "he was as knowing almost as a human being."

"But are you sure his leg is broken?" asked Florence.

"Oh, yes, miss, it is broken safe enough; he has not put his foot to the ground since."

Florence and her friend rode on without saying anything more to Roger.

"We will go and see poor Cap," said the vicar; "I don't believe the leg is really broken. It would take a big stone and a hard blow to break the leg of a big dog like Cap."

"Oh, if you could cure him, how glad Roger would be!" replied Florence.

They soon reached the shepherd's cottage, but the door was fastened; and when they moved the latch, such a furious barking was heard that they drew back, startled. However, a little boy came out of the next cottage, and asked if they wanted to go in, as Roger had left the key with his mother. So the key was got and the door opened and there on the bare brick floor lay the dog, his hair dishevelled, and his eyes sparkling with anger at the intruders. But when he saw the little boy he grew peaceful, and when he looked at Florence and heard her call him "poor Cap," he began to wag his short tail; and then crept from under the table and lay down at her feet. She took hold of one of his paws, patted his old rough head, and talked to him, whilst her friend examined the injured leg. It was dreadfully swollen, and hurt very much to have it examined; but the dog knew it was meant kindly, and though he moaned and winced with pain, he licked the hands that were hurting him.

"It's only a bad bruise, no bones are broken," said her old friend. "Rest is all Cap needs; he will soon be well again."

"I am so glad," said Florence; "but can we do nothing for him, he seems in such pain?"

"There is one thing that would ease the pain and heal the leg all the sooner, and that is plenty of hot water to foment the part."

Florence struck a light with the tinder-box, and lighted the fire, which was already laid. She then set off to the other cottage to get something to bathe the leg with. She found an old flannel petticoat hanging up to dry, and this she carried off, and tore up into strips, which she wrung out in warm water, and laid them tenderly on Cap's swollen leg. It was not long before the poor dog felt the benefit of the application, and he looked grateful, wagging his little stump of a tail in thanks. On their way home they met the shepherd coming slowly along, with a piece of rope in his hand.

"Oh, Roger," cried Florence, "you are not to hang poor old Cap; his leg is not broken at all."

"No, he will serve you yet," said the vicar.

"Well, I be main glad to hear it," said the shepherd, "and thanks to you for going to see him."

On the next morning Florence was up early, and the first thing she did was to take two flannel petticoats to give to the poor woman whose skirt she had torn up to bathe Cap. Then she went to the dog, and was delighted to find the swelling of his leg much less. She bathed it again, and Cap was as grateful as before.

Two or three days afterward Florence and her friend were riding together, when they came up to Roger and his sheep. This time Cap was watching the sheep, though he was lying quite still, and pretending to be asleep. When he heard the voice of Florence speaking to his master, who was portioning out the usual food, his tail wagged and his eyes sparkled, but he did not get up, for he was on duty. The shepherd stopped his work, and as he glanced at the dog with a merry laugh, said, "Do look at the dog, Miss; he be so pleased to hear your voice." Cap's tail went faster and faster. "I be glad," continued the old man, "I did not hang him. I be greatly obliged to you Miss, and the vicar, for what you did. But for you I would have hanged the best dog I ever had in my life."

This child, Florence Nightingale, of whom the foregoing story is told, was born in Florence, Italy, in 1820. Her parents were English, and her early years were given to the studies which a girl fortunately situated would follow. She was taught in science and mathematics as well as in the fluent use of French, German and Italian.

But from the day the little girl nursed the leg of the shepherd's dog, it became the custom of the neighbourhood where she lived to send for her when anyone had a cut or bruise or sick animal. "During her girlhood," says the lady who has written her life, "she was chief almoner to the cottages around her home, and nursed all illnesses under the advice of her mother and the vicar." Her favourite books were those that taught of helpfulness to the suffering and miserable, and it seemed as if her whole nature was turning toward her great work. While still a young girl she became interested in what Elizabeth Fry had done in English prisons, and she paid an interested visit to Mrs. Fry.

When in London she would visit hospitals and kindred institutions, and it is said that in the family travels in Egypt she nursed to health several sick Arabs. Her tastes and time, it is evident, were turned toward a humane and benevolent rather than a social life. Thus passed the years of her younger womanhood.

She had withdrawn from gaieties to learn whatever she could of the hospitals of London, Edinburgh and Dublin, and indeed, of the civil and military hospitals of all Europe, and finally in 1851, she went into training as a nurse in a famous institution at Kaiserwerth on the Rhine. Here, when she had taken the course of instruction, she passed a distinguished examination. After a short period of further study in Paris she returned to her beautiful English home for rest.

But at this time a hospital and home in London for sick and aged governesses was about to fail from lack of means and lack of able direction. To this Miss Nightingale gave herself with ardour, and so renewed its strength that it still remains a witness to her energy. She gave largely to this institution. Nevertheless she was to be found, says a visitor, "organising the nurses, attending to the correspondence, prescriptions and accounts; in short, performing all the duties of a hard-working matron."

Ten years she had been serving apprenticeship for the great work of her life, and now she was thirty-four years old. In 1854 a war broke out between England and Russia. It is known as the Crimean War. England sent her soldiers to the Black Sea in many thousands. These soldiers were sadly clad and fed. Bad management seems to have prevailed, and the service for carrying supplies was inadequate. Warm clothing, blankets, tents and other protection failed to reach the troops. "What a mockery," says one writer, "it must have seemed to the poor fellows, who with scanty rations and in threadbare and tattered clothes, were enduring the most cruel fatigues aggravated by wind and rain and snow and cold upon the bleak heights of the Tauric Chersonese," to hear comforts had been sent them. "When men of courageous mould have been seen 'to weep,' as on night after night, succeeding days of starvation and toil, they were ordered to their work in freezing trenches, who can estimate the exhausting misery they had at first endured?"

"It is now pouring rain," wrote another who was there, "the skies are black as ink—the wind is howling over the staggering tents—the trenches are turned into dykes—in the tents the water is sometimes a foot deep—our men have not either warm or waterproof clothing—they are out for twelve hours at a time in the trenches—they are plunged into the inevitable miseries of a winter campaign—and not a soul seems to care for their comfort, or even for their lives. The wretched beggar who wanders about the streets of London in the rain, leads the life of a prince, compared with the British soldiers who are fighting out here for their country.

"The commonest accessories of a hospital are wanting; there is not the least attention paid to decency or cleanliness; the fetid air can barely struggle out to taint the atmosphere, save through the chinks in the walls and roofs, and, for all I can observe, these men die without the least effort being made to save them. There they lie, just as they were let gently down on the ground by the poor fellows, their comrades, who brought them on their backs from the camp with the greatest tenderness, but who are not allowed to remain with them. The sick appear to be tended by the sick, and the dying by the dying."

During that winter of 1854, many were frozen in their tents. Of nearly forty-five thousand, over eighteen thousand were reported in the hospitals. The English people at last saw their disaster, and certain women volunteered services of helpfulness.

The head of the War Department of the Government who knew of Miss Nightingale's interest in nursing, asked her to superintend and organise a staff of nurses. By a strange coincidence Florence Nightingale had written and offered her aid to the sick and wounded soldiers, and her letter passed the letter from the Government.

It was an undertaking wholly new to English habits—a band of devoted women going to soften the horrors of war and save lives the war had endeavoured to end. As the nurses landed at Boulogne in France, the poor fisherwomen seized and carried their baggage in token of their admiration for the work they were starting out to do. And in their journey through France the innkeepers would not take pay for their lodgings and food. They sailed across the Mediterranean and in November, 1854, reached Scutari, a town in Turkey in Asia, opposite Constantinople.

Four thousand sick and wounded soldiers lay in the hospitals awaiting their ministrations. And still others from a great battle were coming in. These hospitals were so filled that even in the corridors were two rows of mattresses and so close together that two persons could barely walk between the rows. The beds reeked with infection. There was no thought, seemingly, of sanitation. Rather than curers the hospitals were breeders of pestilence.

"The whole of yesterday one could only forget one's own existence," wrote one of the nurses, "for it was spent first in sewing the men's mattresses, and then in washing them, and assisting the surgeons, when we could, in dressing their ghastly wounds after their five days' confinement on board ship, during which space hundreds of wounds had not been dressed. Hundreds of men with fever, dysentery and cholera (the wounded were the smaller portion) filled the wards in succession from the overcrowded transports." Such were the conditions this band of women found.

The head of the band, Miss Nightingale, began her work of organisation. She laboured with tireless energy and indomitable will. But not without opposition. The military and medical officials, says one who was there, "were in the uttermost confusion among themselves, and they generally regarded these gentle missionaries as a new element of anarchy."

As soon as the wounded soldiers had had treatment, Miss Nightingale set in active operations a kitchen where food fit for the sick might be prepared. Many hundreds of the invalids could not eat of ordinary food without serious evil results. In this kitchen the nurses cooked nourishing delicacies for the poor fellows. The following is a little snapshot by one who was there: "In the outer room we caught a glimpse of the justly celebrated Miss Nightingale, an amiable and highly intelligent-looking lady, delicate in form and prepossessing in appearance. Her energies were concentrated for the instant in the careful preparation of a dish of delectable food for an enfeebled patient—one of her homely ministrations to the wan victims of relentless war."

After the kitchen the master—or mistress—mind planned a laundry where the clothing and beds of the sick men might be cleansed. Miss Nightingale, you see, merely organised and conducted housekeeping upon a giant scale. Then in addition she set on foot evening lectures for the men able to listen, and a library and a schoolroom.

Nevertheless she gave distinct and individual service. "I believe," wrote one, "that there never was a severe case of any kind that escaped her notice; and sometimes it was wonderful to see her at the bedside of a patient who had been admitted perhaps but an hour before, and of whose arrival one would hardly have supposed it possible she could already be cognisant."

"As her slender form glided quietly along each corridor every poor fellow's face softens with gratitude at the sight of her," wrote another. "When all the medical officers have retired for the night and silence and darkness have settled down on the miles of prostrate sick, she may be observed alone with a little lamp in her hand making her solitary rounds. No one who has observed her fragile figure and delicate health can avoid misgivings lest these should fail. With the heart of a true woman and the manners of a lady she combines a surprising calmness of judgment and promptitude and decision of character."

"To see her pass was happiness," one poor fellow said. "As she passed down the beds she would nod to one and smile at many more; but she could not do it to all, you know. We lay there by hundreds; but we could kiss her shadow as it fell, and lay our heads upon the pillows again, content."

"The magic of her power over men used often to be felt," wrote Kinglake the historian, "in the room—the dreaded, the blood-stained room—where 'operations' took place. There perhaps the maimed soldier, if not yet resigned to his fate, might at first be craving death rather than meet the knife of the surgeon; but when such a one looked and saw that the honoured lady-in-chief was patiently standing by him and, with lips closely set and hands folded, decreeing herself to go through the pain of witnessing pain, he used to fall into the mood of obeying the silent command, and, finding strange support in her presence, bring himself to submit and endure."

Every fresh detachment of the wounded meant fresh work for the band of devoted women. Miss Nightingale was always among the busiest and she was known to stand for twenty hours assisting at operations, directing nurses, herself ministering to cholera and fever patients and distributing stores. Once she was prostrated by fever for some weeks. Illness also attacked others of the nurses and many were laid in quiet graves in that distant land.

At last the fighting was brought to an end. For a year and a half had the noble and humane work of nursing gone on and shown the world how much greater is the saving of lives than the destruction of lives by the murder of war. The gratitude the English people felt for what the nurses had done they expressed by a gift of fifty thousand pounds to Miss Nightingale after her return to England. They had planned also a public welcome of their heroine, but with the modesty and calm judgment that always characterised her, she slipped quietly into England by the carriage of a French steamer and so to her country home. Queen Victoria, who with her husband the Prince Consort, had most earnestly admired Miss Nightingale's course, and had sought direct knowledge of her work during her stay in the East, entertained her at Balmoral and presented her with a valuable jewel. The sum presented her by the nation was, at her request, given to the foundation of a training home for nurses in connection with St. Thomas's Hospital. It is called the "Nightingale Home."

This "Angel of the Crimea" returned to England so enfeebled with arduous labour that she has never since entered active life. She lived many years, perforce, in her own sick-room with scarcely strength to pen a letter, and saw no one but closest associates. The knowledge and experience she had got in public service, however, she gave to the world in part in her "Notes on Nursing" and "Notes on Hospitals," and other publications. Several Governments have sought her advice upon the sanitation of army camps, and the Red Cross Society is in part from her aid and endeavour.

Her "Notes on Nursing" are full of sound sense and we should be more fortunate if the knowledge in them were more general than it is.

"Everything you do in a patient's room after he is 'put up' for the night increases tenfold the risk of his having a bad night; but if you rouse him up after he has fallen asleep, you do not risk—you secure him a bad night."

"Conciseness and decision are above all things necessary with the sick. Let your doubt be to yourself, your decision to them."

"Above all leave the sick-room quietly, and come into it quietly; not suddenly, not with a rush."

"Remember never to lean against, sit upon, or unnecessarily shake the bed upon which a patient lies."

"An extraordinary fallacy is the dread of night air," she wrote. "What air can we breathe at night but night air? The choice is between pure night air from without and foul night air from within. Most people prefer the latter—an unaccountable choice. What will they say if it be proved true that fully one-half of all the disease we suffer from is occasioned by people sleeping with their windows shut? An open window most nights of the year can never hurt anyone. In great cities night air is often the best and purest to be had in the twenty-four hours."

"The five essentials, for healthy houses," she again says, "are pure air, pure water, efficient drainage, cleanliness and light. I have known whole houses and hospitals smell of the sink. I have met just as strong a stream of sewer air coming up the back staircase of a grand London house, from the sink, as I have ever met at Scutari; and I have seen the rooms in that house all ventilated by the open doors, and the passages all unventilated by the close windows, in order that as much of the sewer air as possible might be conducted into and retained in the bedrooms. It is wonderful!"

She is opposed to dark houses; says they promote scrofula; to old papered walls and to carpets full of dust. An uninhabited room becomes full of foul air soon, and needs to have the windows open often. She would keep sick people, or well, forever in the sunlight if possible, for sunlight is the greatest possible purifier of the atmosphere. "In the unsunned sides of narrow streets," she writes, "there is degeneracy and weakliness of the human race—mind and body equally degenerating. Oh, the crowded school, where so many children's epidemics have their origin, what a tale its air test would tell!"

"Nursing is an art; and if it is to be made an art, requires as exclusive a devotion, as hard a preparation, as any painter's or sculptor's work; for what is the having to do with dead canvas or cold marble compared with having to do with the living body, the temple of God's Spirit? Nursing is one of the fine arts; I had almost said, the finest of the fine arts."

Miss Nightingale is living with her great work done. Still she continues and will ever continue, her ministrations in the bravery, devotion and unselfishness of every nurse and in the effective work of every hospital.

SANTA FILOMENA

BY HENRY WADSWORTH LONGFELLOW

When e'er a noble deed is wrought, When e'er is spoken a noble thought, Our hearts in glad surprise, To higher levels rise.

The tidal wave of deeper souls Into our inmost being rolls, And lifts us unawares Out of all meaner cares.

Honour to those whose words or deeds Thus help us in our daily needs, And by their overflow Raise us from what is low!

Thus thought I, as by night I read Of the great army of the dead, The trenches cold and damp, The starved and frozen camp.

The wounded from the battle-plain, In dreary hospitals of pain, The cheerless corridors, The cold and stony floors.

Lo! in that house of misery A lady with a lamp I see Pass through the glimmering gloom And flit from room to room.

And slow, as in a dream of bliss The speechless sufferer turns to kiss Her shadow as it falls Upon the darkening walls.

As if a door in heaven should be Opened and then closed suddenly The vision came and went The light shone and was spent

On England's annals, through the long Hereafter of her speech and song, That light its rays shall cast From the portals of the past.

A Lady with a Lamp shall stand, In the great history of the land, A noble type of good, Heroic womanhood.

Nor even shall be wanting here The palm, the lily and the spear The symbols that of yore Saint Filomena[3] bore.

---

[3] In her "Sacred and Legendary Art," Mrs. Jamieson writes that "at Pisa the Church of San Francesco contained a chapel dedicated to Santa Filomena; over the altar is a picture by Sabatelli, representing the saint as a beautiful nymph-like figure floating down from heaven, attended by two angels, bearing the lily, palm, and javelin, and beneath,

in the foreground, the sick and maimed who are healed by her intercession."

Longfellow gave the name Filomena to Florence Nightingale partly because of her labours among the sick and dying at Scutari, and partly on account of the resemblance between Filomena and the Latin Philomela (nightingale).—*Brewer*.

www.ingramcontent.com/pod-product-compliance
Lightning Source LLC
Chambersburg PA
CBHW051645260626
47170CB00004B/1334